The Trading Athlete

The Trading Athlete

Winning the Mental Game of Online Trading

SHANE MURPHY, PH.D.

DOUG HIRSCHHORN, M.S.

John Wiley & Sons, Inc.

New York • Chichester • Weinheim • Brisbane • Singapore • Toronto

Published by John Wiley & Sons, Inc.
Published simultaneously in Canada.

This publication is designed to provide accurate and authoritative information in
regard to the subject matter covered. It is sold with the understanding that the
publisher is not engaged in rendering professional services. If professional advice or
other expert assistance is required, the services of a competent professional person
should be sought.

Library of Congress Cataloging-in-Publication Data:

Murphy, Shane M., 1957–
      The trading athlete: winning the mental game of online trading / Shane Murphy
   & Doug Hirschhorn.
         p. cm.
      Includes index.
      ISBN 0-471-41870-6 (cloth : alk. paper)
       1. Electronic trading of securities. I. Hirschhorn, Doug. II. Title.

   HG4515.95 .M87 2001
   332.64'0285'4678--dc21

                                                              2001026191

10 9 8 7 6 5 4 3 2 1

To Audrey Finkelstein,
    You are the true definition of excellence.
In memory of Charles Finkelstein,
    You will always be my hero.

—Doug Hirschhorn

ACKNOWLEDGMENTS

Many thanks to Doug, who was a powerhouse on this project. And, as always, love and thanks to my family, Annemarie, Bryan, and Theresa, for supporting me in my writing.

—Shane Murphy

Special thanks to my parents, Evie and Joel. Mom, for always being my #1 fan—here's your first "Hi Mom!" Dad, for teaching me those three important life lessons before I played in my first baseball game. I love you both for always knowing that I would hit a homerun in the game of life.

Thank you to Teri Loughead for showing me my wings; to Sid Kaz for teaching me how to trade and for being a friend when I needed one; to my partner and mentor, Shane Murphy for taking a chance on me years ago; and to our editor, Claudio Campuzano, for his guidance in putting this book together.

Thanks to some of the Trading Athletes who gave us feedback along the way: Dave Keyt, Matt "Squiggy" Palazzolo, and Josh Winstral. Dave, I am still a better golfer than you are. Squiggy, it's a good thing you are better at trading than you were at baseball. And Josh, your success as a trader has inspired us all.

And finally, and most importantly to my wife, Amy. Thank you for your patience, love, and support as I continue to pursue my dreams. I love you.

—Doug Hirschhorn

PREFACE

A few years ago we came to the surprising conclusion that the world of online trading obeys most of the same rules as the world of competitive sports. We found that the methods and strategies of sport psychology, which we knew so well, could be applied to the trading game with equal success. At first we worked with some individual clients, showing them how to apply sport psychology principles to enhance their trading effectiveness. Because that approach was very successful, we were asked to work with several companies, and train their staff in our sport psychology approach. Once again the people we worked with enjoyed great success thanks to the application of our methods. And so we began to offer workshops on the sport psychology of trading, and eventually, decided to write this book to share our methods with the widest possible audience. The beauty of our "sport psychology approach to trading" is that whether you are a rookie or an all star in the trading game, whether you trade from home, in a trading house, or even on a trading floor, you will be able to apply our winning methods to your current game plan. We are confident that by the time you have finished this book, you will be convinced, as we are, that you are an online trading athlete, and that diligent application of the principles of sport psychology will help you take your game to the next level as you achieve your potential as a trader.

Keep your eye on the ball and your head in the game!

—Shane Murphy and Doug Hirschhorn

CONTENTS

* Worrying About the Future
* Unhappiness with the Present
* Playing One Trade at a Time
* The 10-Minute Promise
* Focus on Your Goals

THE MENTAL GAME OF TRADING

WHAT IS AN ONLINE TRADING ATHLETE?

Well, we know what an athlete is, and we know the many challenges they face in the world of competition. An online trader faces the same challenges, although in a different environment, and benefits from having the same disciplined mental approach to trading that an athlete has to sports.

Perhaps some concrete examples will make this clearer. Let us take a look at some of the challenges faced by competitive athletes on an everyday basis.

- A wide receiver in football must be fast and strong, able to evade would-be tacklers, run downfield and catch a ball thrown with great speed by a quarterback, and survive fearsome hits by opposing linebackers.
- A baseball player must be able to face a ball thrown at more than 90 miles per hour by a pitcher standing on a mound just over 60 feet away, reacting in a split second and deciding whether to swing or let the ball go by.

- A cyclist must be in amazing physical shape, able to withstand not only the rigors of riding many miles every day to train for an event, but also to go at top speed during a race, jostling against dozens of other riders for good position in the peleton, and then be able to summon one last burst of energy to separate from the pack over the last hundred meters before the finish line.

These physical challenges are fearsome, and athletes work with strength coaches, nutritional experts, exercise physiologists, and sports medicine specialists to get their bodies in shape to meet them.

But another part of the challenge for athletes is mental. They must have the self-discipline to get up early in the morning to do the extra training required to become a champion; they must set long-term goals so they know their ultimate destination, but also be able to focus on short-term stepping-stone goals along the way; they must have the courage to enter competitions, despite not knowing the eventual outcome, and the inner strength to try again, even after bitter defeat; and they must have the resolve to stay focused despite the distractions offered by their most challenging opponent—themselves. It is in an athlete's own mind that many of the hardest games are played overcoming the self-doubt of "Am I good enough?"; bouncing back from the self-criticism of "You idiot, you messed up again!"; and persevering despite the inner voice that says "You'll never make it, you don't have what it takes, why don't you quit right now and go home and relax?" All athletes know that their toughest opponents are themselves—a far more relentless and inescapable opponent than any that takes the field or the court against them.

Sport psychology is the field that has grown to study these mental aspects of sport. Sport psychologists study the game that takes place between the ears, the inner game that makes the critical difference between winning and losing. By researching the effectiveness of various mental approaches to sports, it has been possible to determine strategies that promote athletic success and in any competitive situation, this valuable information is oftentimes called the "edge." The role of sport psychologists is to pass this information on to coaches and athletes and this book is designed to pass it on to you.

We believe that our combined approach to the world of online trading offers you a unique and exciting approach to achieving success. Think of it as your own personalized "one-two punch." Our ideas have been tested and proven with both elite athletes and with successful traders. That is why we ask all those who work in the world of trading, stock-broking, and investing to think of themselves as *athletes*. No, you are not taking the field in a uniform in front of thousands of cheering fans to face an opponent determined to smash you into a thousand pieces. But if you look at it from our perspective, you are playing a game, even though the stakes are high, in a very competitive environment where many others are also seeking to gain an advantage over you. If you think of yourself as an online trading athlete, we believe that you will gain a fresh perspective that will thoroughly prepare you for the rigors and demands of the world of online trading.

THE MENTAL CHALLENGES FACED BY BOTH ATHLETES AND ONLINE TRADERS

What do athletes share in common with online traders? Think about the situations faced by athletes and the mental skills required to be successful in those situations. Below we list some of these common challenges faced by competitive athletes. Then we look at situations typically faced by online traders, so you can see how their situations are similar to those from the athletic world.

- Athletes face suddenly changing conditions on the field or the court, such as when an opponent hits a homerun, intercepts a pass, or blows past them on the court. They need to make quick decisions about what to do to stay in the game.
- Online traders face suddenly changing conditions in the market, such as when one position suddenly begins to tank, while another starts to rise. They need to make quick decisions about the right course of action to take to stay profitable.

- Athletes face the demand of attaining excellent performance consistently. In the course of a season, a baseball or football team must win consistently to have a chance of making the playoffs. A tour golfer must earn enough money over the course of a season to keep their tour card for the following season.
- Online traders must be consistently successful to stay in business. Frequently they are the main bread-winner for their families, so the pressure is on to achieve at a high level. If they sustain too many losses, they may eventually have to find another career.

- Athletes need to analyze large amounts of information very rapidly to make precise decisions about what to do. A quarterback on a football team drops back in the pocket to pass and must rapidly scan his primary and secondary receivers to see which one is open, while maintaining a peripheral sense of who is near him in

order to avoid the blitzing 240-pound linebacker trying to crush him. A good decision and the receiver
breaks free for a 50-yard touchdown. A bad decision
and the other team returns an interception back for a
touchdown of their own.

- Online traders need to analyze large amounts of information very rapidly to make effective decisions
about when to trade, with what stock, and in what
amounts. Depending on their overall strategy, they
must pay attention to order flow, earnings reports, sector performances, trading history, current news, economic trends, interest rate movements, and a host of
other influential variables that will guide their
choices. A good decision and they have initiated a winning trade. A bad decision and weeks of hard work and
profits can go down the drain.

- Athletes face constant pressure. It comes from many
sides, in many forms: the coach who is a demanding
perfectionist; the fans who hunger for a long-awaited
championship; the media who seek out a hint of weakness to feast on controversy; and teammates who expect the same commitment and intensity, the same
blood and sweat, that they are prepared to offer.

- Online traders face constant pressure. It also comes
from many sides, in many forms: the unyielding structure of the trading day, with a set opening and closing
and hours of frenetic activity in between; the constant
flow of information, indicating huge profits to be
made if the right choices are acted on; colleagues and
rivals who are successful, inspiring some jealousy, and
those who fail, triggering fearful thoughts of a common fate; and the market itself, a behemoth that is impossible to predict, and which is brutal to those un-
prepared for its vagaries.

- Athletes must put in countless hours of solid practice and preparation to ready themselves for great performances. When no one else is awake, they get up early and take to the rink or the field or the track to put in the long hours required for competitive success at the elite level. When the other athletes have gone home, the great champions stay behind, making a few more putts, taking a few more serves, swimming another lap or two—whatever it takes to stay one step ahead of the competition. And even when the grueling physical workouts are over, athletes must mentally ready themselves for the stress of competition, for facing an opponent who wants it as badly as they do, and for coping with the inevitable wins and losses of competitive sports.

- Online traders must spend hours and hours preparing themselves for the demands of the trading day. Whether it is researching a new market sector, intensely studying an individual stock, learning a new analytical technique, or just the hard work of staying current in their area, they must prepare, prepare, prepare. Even when the preparation is done, there still remains the mental preparation necessary to handle the emotional stresses of a trading day, with its ups and downs, its triumphs and disasters.

As you can see, although the setting is different and the nature of the competition is different, there are a tremendous number of similarities in the challenges faced by athletes and traders on a daily basis. These challenges require the same mental skills to overcome. For this reason, we think of the traders we work with as athletes—online trading athletes. Our expertise combines both sport psychology and trading, and this gives us a unique insight into the world of trading. We have found that the strategies and concepts of sport psychology are readily applicable to online trading and can make a huge difference in results.

You should think of this book as your personal guide to becoming a successful online trading athlete. Our approach is not a quick fix, but rather a carefully designed formula drawing from proven sport psychology strategies and real-life trading experiences to help online trading athletes reach their individual level of performance excellence (see Figure A).

FIGURE A   ACHIEVING PERFORMANCE EXCELLENCE

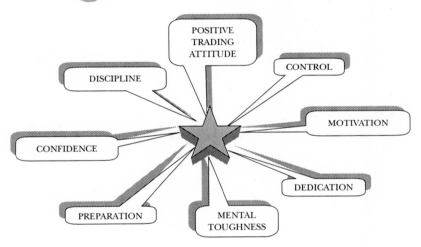

With all of this said, get your game face on, pick up your bat and let's "play ball."

A STUDY IN EXCELLENCE:
CATHY FREEMAN

At the Summer Olympic Games in Sydney in 2000, several performances stood out among a host of achievements as worthy of special mention: Marion Jones and her three

(continued)

gold medals; Michael Johnson and another superb performance in the 400 meters; and Peter VanHogenboom, the amazing Dutch swimmer who set new world records and claimed Olympic gold in both the 100 and 200 meters. But one athlete captured our attention, not only for her medal-winning achievement, but also for the way she competed. Cathy Freeman was almost the symbol of the 2000 Games. She was chosen to light the Olympic torch at the Opening Ceremonies in Stadium Australia, an emotion-charged moment that paid tribute not only to a great athlete, but also to the sad history of the native people who were brutally treated by colonizing Europeans for 200 years. Cathy Freeman is an aborigine, a member of the culture that inhabited Australia for thousands of years before the Europeans arrived in the 18th century, but who were pushed almost to extinction before they made a stand for independence and recognition by the colonizing immigrants. Cathy Freeman's selection as the torchlighter was symbolic, and surely deeply meaningful to her, as an outspoken champion of aboriginal rights.

What a dramatic night it was, then, nearly a week later, when she took her place at the starting line of the women's 400-meter race. Not only was she representing the aborigine people, but she carried the hopes and expectations of an entire country on her slim shoulders. Australians are a sports-mad people (we should know, Shane was born and raised there), who love their champions fiercely. All 20 million of them knew that their nation's best chance for a track and field gold medal at their hometown Olympic Games rested with the heart and soul of this young champion. We have seen many, many great sporting moments, but we cannot remember any stadium filled with such an inundation of noise, nor had we ever seen so many explosions of light, so many cameras flashing as they captured the moment! Surely none of us can imagine the pressure she felt before the race. We cannot imagine what went through her head: the possibilities of glory; the thoughts of a misstep or stumble and painful defeat. We only know that most of us would not want to be in her shoes.

Of course, the story had a happy ending. At the final turn there were two runners ahead of her, and it seemed for a moment that perhaps she would be overwhelmed by the crushing weight of a country's expectations. But Cathy Freeman came roaring down the straight, bringing the huge stadium roaring to life, and at the finish she seemed to have moved into a higher gear than any other runner, speeding away from them and toward Olympic immortality. Yet, when the race ended, the true pressure on her showed for a few moments as she collapsed to the ground and sat with her head between her knees, as if the magnitude of her accomplishment had just suddenly caught up with her. It took a few minutes, but finally she recovered, and she was Cathy again, a huge smile on her face, draped in flags and waving to her worldwide audience.

The ability to handle that sort of pressure and still perform to your potential is exactly what we are talking about in this book. You may never be asked to run 400-meters in under 50 seconds, but as an online trading athlete you will face many, many moments of truth, when you are asked to make a split-second decision with some significant financial consequences on the line. To highlight the importance of the mental game

(continued)

in preparing for your own moments of truth, it is instructive to read the words of Cathy Freeman, describing her approach to running and to competition. As you read her comments below, you will understand the critical importance of the mental game. It is this same approach, a disciplined mental and emotional approach, based on the knowledge base of sport psychology that we want you to learn to bring to your trading.

"I know what works for me before a race. I don't freak out. I know exactly what I need to do. I think I know myself now."

"I'm not intimidated by these other world class athletes. I slide into the picture. I'm a racer. I get a real buzz out of it."

"My focusing skills are much better. I'm a lot more in control."

"I make sure my mind is at peace before I get out on the track."

"I practice over and over in my head what I have to do. If I'm walking out relaxed on the track it's because I know exactly what I need to do."

"You don't let anything blur your vision or complicate things: it's all focus."

"There is so much more to my running than just lining up at the start and running around. There are emotional, personal things. They motivate me, get my emotional juices stirred up inside me, help me channel my emotions into running."

"I know it makes my family happy to see me making something of my life. I know what I'm doing does touch their lives."

KEEPING IT IN PERSPECTIVE

Let us face it, trading is a 50-50 game. You can look at all the charts, graphs, earning reports, summaries, and estimates you want but when push comes to shove and the bell rings, it is just a 50-50 game. Stocks either go up or they go down. You do not care which way as long as they go (and as long as you are on the right side). Instead of pushing or forcing, relax, focus, identify the momentum, and hold on for the ride. Avoid staying on too long. Remember there is always another ride waiting when this one is over. After all, you are trading. What does that really mean to you? Think about it. Trading means buying and selling. You have no long-term vested interest in the company, no retirement plan to pay into, no management to impress, you are not even sending them a resume for a job. You are an online trader.

You want to be in and out, taking fractions or even chunks of a point each time. If a company goes bankrupt tomorrow, you do not care (unless you are short it) because there is always another game going on somewhere in the market. So with this in mind, instead of looking at it as a business, see it from the athlete's point of view. After all, day trading is just another competitive game, right? And because it is a game, think of yourself as an online trading athlete and take a game approach.

When it is the bottom of the ninth inning, with two outs, and you are on deck, are you the kind of hitter who wants to be up to bat with the winning run on third or are you hoping that the player in front of you makes the last out? Are you the kind of basketball player who wants the ball when the score is tied and there are three seconds left on the clock? Are you the kind of golfer who can drain that 10-foot put to save par when you are down a stroke? If you are praying you do not get up to the plate or that the ball is not passed to you or that your opponent duffs his or her shot so you can have some cushion, then online trading is probably not for you because in this game, a lack of confidence and discipline is going to cost you. If you feel that you used to be that hitter or basketball player or golfer and somehow lost the touch somewhere along the way, do not hit the showers just yet, let us see if we can work through it together. After all, you had that magic touch at one point in time, so where did it go? You are still the same person, right? Of course you are. Your mind set has simply changed and along with it your confidence, discipline, and motivation. This book is designed to help you realize it and find it again so you can get back into the lineup and start winning some games.

Instead of a ball, it is "penny" or "quarter" or "point." Instead of a bat or club, you have a keyboard. Instead of swinging, you are placing orders for 1,000 shares. Want to take a bigger swing? Looking for that homerun or that hole in one? Then you change your order size to 5,000 or 10,000 shares. Having an off day and not feeling your rhythm? Then pick up a lighter bat or use your seven iron and move your trades down to 100 or 300 shares at a time. Lay down a few bunts or find your swing so you can get your timing back.

You are not the first person ever to trade the market, and you are certainly not the first person to try making a living doing it. We suggest you avoid being the next person to take those big homerun swings, which may cause you to strike out like Casey in "Casey at the Bat." Remember, "there is no joy in Mudville." Do not worry if you often feel that you have missed a big opportunity: the market is not going to disappear. It will still be there tomorrow. Money will be waiting for you there. Patience. The trick is to make sure that you can afford to put the uniform on when it is game time again.

We recently spoke to an experienced trader who has participated in several "boom" markets, when certain sectors seemed to be "on fire" creating "can't miss" trading opportunities. The most recent example of this was the technology and "dot com" boom of the late 1990s. His comment summed up for us the psychology of this boom mentality. "It's weird, there were often days when I had made a lot of money, more money than I ever typically made in a trading day, and yet I felt depressed at the close of the day. I felt left behind. I would hear stories of all the money being made and I felt that I was missing out. I could sense these fabulous opportunities out there and it seemed as if I wasn't doing enough, I wasn't getting my share. It's weird looking back. Here I was making great money and I felt terrible."

Avoid falling into the same trap of constantly comparing yourself to others, or to the "best case" scenario. Yes, there is lots of money to be made trading, under the right conditions. There is also lots of ways to lose money, even in a boom market. What we will ask of you in this book is to develop a discipline, a trust in your own game plan, so that you will be confident for the long-term, and not be a one-week wonder. No matter how you slice it, some things will never change. Online trading is a game (a 50-50 one at that). The sun will set tonight and rise tomorrow and along with it the market will close today and reopen tomorrow. The only question that remains is, do you have the motivation, confidence, and discipline to put the uniform back on, get into the lineup, and step up to the plate when the umpire yells "Play ball"?

There is no guarantee that you are going to be a wildly successful online trading athlete, but at least give yourself the best chance possible to succeed when you step onto that tee box. That is the lesson we have learned from sport psychology: the best athletes do everything in their power to put themselves in a position to win, and then they focus and enjoy the competition. Just as the final outcome is something that the athlete cannot control, because it depends on multiple factors, the final outcome is something you cannot control, because you can never control the market. But you can learn to put yourself into the best position to win, day in and day out. By drawing from the athletic perspective of competition and success we know we can help you reach your potential every time you step up to the plate to make a trade.

To help you understand just what we are talking about, here is a collection of quotes from successful online trading athletes who consistently reach their potential in the trading game.

LESSONS FROM THE FIELD

"It's easy to dream about the future, but I have found that I am most consistent when I concentrate on the current trade. I view each trade I make like a single brick in a house that I am trying to build."

"I always write down my daily goals before the market opens and then I imagine what it will feel like at the end of the day when I reach them. This helps me focus on what I need to do."

"I always try to stay patient and in control so that when my indicators appear, I can react and attack. Wait for it. There it is. Go for it. That's my motto."

"Right before big numbers come out, I feel myself tense up. So I stop, focus on my breathing and relax so that I can make those split-second decisions without hesitating."

"Sometimes it just feels like I am buying the low and selling the high. That's when I really focus because I know that I am on top of my game."

"If I get upset after a trade, I take a quick time-out. I leave my trading stadium. I get up and walk around until I cool down. It's dangerous for me to be in the game if I'm feeling angry."

"It's amazing. When things aren't going my way I just sit up straight, keep my head up and shoulders back, and I feel a positive charge run through my body."

"When the opening bell rings, I am all about business. I don't eat, chit-chat, or read magazines. I am here to trade."

Now ask yourself: "Do these qualities describe the type of trader I am or the type of trader I want to be?"

If you are hearing yourself in these lessons from the field, then keep up the good work. However, if you feel that you are not reaching your potential as a trader, then you have picked up the right book. You see, trading is a competitive game and our book is written for the athlete—the online trading athlete. You do not have to have played sports yourself to benefit from this book, although if you are a former athlete then you will surely recognize some of the strategies and approaches we describe. But if you are not, then do not sweat it; either way our challenge to all of our readers is to start to think like an athlete—an online trading athlete.

CHAPTER ONE

THE MENTAL KEYS TO BECOMING A MASTERFUL ONLINE TRADING ATHLETE

Do you believe that champions are just born that way, or do you believe that champions earn their success through application of talent? If you said that champions have to earn it, congratulations, we are on the same page. If you said that champions are born that way, we hope to convince you that you are wrong. You see, over the years we have seen many talented players who do not achieve what they are capable of and it has nothing to do with their talent level. Instead, it has everything to do with their commitment, their goals, and their focus. For every champion who makes it to the NBA, NFL, MLB, and so on, there are many equally talented athletes who drop out along the way. Champions become great through applying certain fundamental principles to their lives.

There are tons of people who could be great, but they don't practice the basics. They don't want to work at it.

—Michael Jordan, quoted on his return
to the Chicago Bulls, March 27, 1995.

1

Sport psychologists have studied in depth the factors that make up long-term success. Our goal in this book is to show you what we have learned about success, and how to apply it to your world of online trading. We will assume that you have the talent and desire to be a successful online trading athlete. We will go beyond that and show you that what you think about, the goals you set, what you choose to focus on, and your attitude toward trading will be the final factors that decide how successful you are.

GETTING STARTED— MOTIVATION

In the next chapter, we discuss in depth the art of goal setting, and show you why being good at that skill is critical for successful trading. At the heart of goal setting is having a dream. All of the Olympic athletes whom we work with begin with a dream. There is something they want out of their sporting participation. The dream varies from individual to individual. For one athlete it is the dream of being the best in the world at what he does; for another it is the dream of representing her country at the Olympic Games; and for another it is the dream of doing something he loves and has fun with every day for the next four years. The athletes tell us that when things get rough, when they experience a setback, when they feel like giving up, it is the dream that keeps them going. They think about their dream and they just do not want to let it die, they cannot bear to give it up. So they struggle on, giving it one more try, and very often another, and often yet another, until the dream is fulfilled.

What is your dream as an online trading athlete? If you do not have one, what is going to keep you going when things get rough? What will sustain you when the market turns against you, when you have a terrible month, when your friends quit, or when you seem to lack the energy to keep going? It is easy to be focused and happy when everything is going well. What makes a champion is that they have persevered through the hard times, so that when opportunity presents itself, they know how important their chance is. For example, in 1998 and 1999, quarterback John Elway won the Super Bowl with the Denver Broncos, the ultimate achievement for any football player. But in 1986, 1987, and 1990, he lost the Super Bowl, each time in disastrous, almost humiliating fashion. As he got older the bumps and bruises of an NFL career began to multiply, and he must have asked himself many times whether it was worthwhile to continue. But he had the dream of winning the Super Bowl, and this sustained him through the hardest times until he fulfilled his ambition.

Not every dream comes true, but the interesting thing is that the retired athletes we have spoken to are happy that they pursued their dream, whether it became a reality or not. "I never won that Olympic medal," says Jan, a figure skater. "But the places I've been, the people I've met, are all due to that dream. I can't bear to think of how empty my life might have been without it." Another athlete commented, "Yes, I would have given anything to go to the Olympic Games. Being so close was very hard to take. But then again, I realize now how much I've grown from my experience. I learned an awful lot during those 10 years. I certainly wouldn't give back a single minute of that time."

For some of you, the answer to the question "What is my dream as a trader?" is an easy one. You already have a vivid picture in your mind of what you want to accomplish in your trading career. But for others reading this book, this is a tough question. We want you to take your time with it, because the answer is very important. And your dreams will be very, very important in shaping the goals you set in the next chapter.

> *You can't hit a target you cannot see and you cannot see a target you do not have.*

—Zig Ziglar

If you are drawing a blank right now, begin by asking yourself, "Why am I trading?" Is it for the money, the freedom, the thrill, or to escape from doing something else? Did you start because a friend started trading, or because you read a magazine article about trading, or because you have expertise in finances or stocks? There is no right answer to this question, but it is very important that you have an answer. If you cannot answer the question "Why am I trading?" you are destined to be like a ship without a rudder. Your trading will drift aimlessly, and based on our experience and observations, you are unlikely to enjoy any long-term success. Our work in sport psychology has taught us that those who achieve great things are those who have great goals. They know where they are going. As you begin to think about and describe your dream, you are on your way to being able to develop your own personal trading mission statement. This statement will be a valuable resource in your efforts to master the mental game of online trading.

You have probably heard a lot about mission statements over the past few years. They seem to have become trendy, and for a good reason: they work! What might surprise you is that it is not only big corporations that have mission statements. Top athletes and high performers in other fields often personalize their goals through specific mission statements as well. A mission statement organizes your goals into a clear statement of purpose and helps remind you every day of why you enjoy trading and what your trading objectives are. As an online trading athlete, it is up to you to find your mission, your purpose, your reason for "Why am I trading?"

It is only possible to coach effectively if you are doing something you truly enjoy. It's difficult to win doing something you don't enjoy.

—Joe Paterno

Mission statements should be clear, brief, and personalized. Every statement for every trader will be different. Take some time to fully work out your motives for being a trader. Once you are able to put your mission statement down on paper it will serve as the bedrock to your future success as an online trading athlete. To help you develop the basics of a personal trading mission statement, complete the following exercise.

A) Write down what you think your top three strengths are as a trader.

1. _____

2. _____

3. _____

B) Write down three qualities you would like to have, or aspects of your trading you want to improve on.

1. _____

2. _____

3. _____

C) Now write down three things that you can expect if you are successful as an online trading athlete

1. _____

2. _____

3. _____

To complete your first mission statement, fill in the blanks below with your answers to the questions above:

"I am ____A____. My goal as an online trading athlete is to ____B____. By sticking to my game plan, I will accomplish ____C____."

Here are some examples of how traders we know have used the above exercise to develop their own personal trading mission statements. First are the answers from Debbie, an experienced trader who spent six years in various aspects of customer relations with a financial services institution, trading part-time, before she became a full-time trader. Debbie was also a nationally ranked tennis player in college. Here are her answers to these questions:

A) Write down what you think your top three strengths are.

1. I am a competitive athlete
2. I have a strong work ethic
3. I enjoy working with people

B) Write down three qualities you would like to have or improve on.

1. More discipline

2. Have more fun trading
3. Show more patience

C) Now write down three things that you can expect if you are successful as an online trading athlete

1. Financial security
2. Recognition from peers
3. Satisfaction in my career choice

DEBBIE'S PERSONAL TRADING MISSION STATEMENT

"I am a competitive online trading athlete. My goal is to be disciplined and patient every time I step up to serve in the trading game. I will enjoy my time trading. Sticking to my personal game plan will enable me to become an all-star and achieve financial success."

Notice that when she completed her mission statement, Debbie was able to identify clearly why she was trading. However, she did not write this statement on her first attempt. It took several months of thought and self-discovery to understand why she was in the trading game. Once she got to this version, she found that it made sense to her and kept her focused when she was having an off day or when she fell into a slump. We will discuss dealing with slumps and setbacks in detail in Chapters 3 and 4, but realize that the ability to deal with failures begins with the self-knowledge that you are doing something worthwhile, something that makes you not want to give up easily.

Here is another example of the process of constructing a personal trading mission statement, this time from a rookie trader, Joel, who was 45 when he retired as a fireman and took up trading as an occupation.

A) Write down what you think your top three strengths are.

1. I am strong and determined
2. I am willing to sacrifice to get what I want
3. I enjoy life

B) Write down three qualities you would like to have or improve on.

1. I want to know more about trading
2. I do not want to gamble
3. I need more confidence

C) Now write down three things that you can expect if you are successful as an online trading athlete.

1. I will make a nest egg for my retirement years
2. I will be knowledgeable
3. I will impress my buddies

JOEL'S PERSONAL TRADING MISSION STATEMENT

"I am a strong, determined trader and I will commit myself to being the best trader I can be. My goal as on online trading athlete is to be smart, prudent, and confident. I will make a game plan, stick to it, and enjoy working hard until I retire."

You can immediately see how Joel's statement is vastly different from Debbie's, and how it is a reflection of his unique personality and his approach to life. The bottom line is a good mission statement is what works for you.

Over time, we change, or trading skills change, and so our mission statements must change. Be willing to add or alter your mission statement as you grow in your career as an online trading athlete. We suggest an annual end-of-the-year review of your personal mission statement to see if it needs updating.

Now that you have committed your first mission statement to paper make sure you post it over your "trading stadium" (desk area) so that you can read it whenever you need to remind yourself of your purpose and objectives. (To find out more about how to set up your own Winner's Trading Stadium, see Appendix A, Extra Innings, beginning on page 219 in the back of this book.)

LONG-TERM SUCCESS—INNER MOTIVATION

Understanding why you trade is the first step to becoming a successful trader, but it is just a beginning. To be truly successful over the long haul, you need to examine your motivations more carefully and begin to understand that there are differences between doing something in order to get a payoff, and doing something because you want to be good at it. Although we all like to receive some reward for doing a good job, sport psychologists have found that athletes are actually more successful when they stop focusing all their energies on trying to win, and learn to focus on being excellent at what they do. Does this sound confusing? It might at first, but the concept is actually very simple. There is a big difference between looking good and actually being good.

Some of your motivations for being a trader are external to you (financial reward, recognition from colleagues) while others are more internal to you (the rush you get from competing, the satisfaction of having mastered a new approach to trading). What we have found are that these internal motivations are what sustain you when things get hard. If a situation is difficult and challenging, and your motivation is purely external, there is a tendency to give up or look for the easy way out. But if your motivation is internal, the difficult and challenging way is actually the most satisfying. Those with a strong inner motivation seek out challenges so that they can keep pushing themselves to be better.

Sport psychologists call this the difference between an ego approach to competition and a mastery approach. Let us look at the differences.

Someone with an ego approach to trading:

- Wants to be thought of as a successful trader
- Wants to win
- Compares themselves to other traders
- Is scared of losing
- Wants to look good
- Does not care how they win, as long as they do

Someone with a mastery approach to trading:

- Wants to be an excellent trader
- Is always looking for ways to improve
- Does not worry about the performance of other traders
- Is not satisfied with a good outcome if their approach was flawed
- Does not like to lose, but learns from every setback
- Wants to be good

Why is this important? It is important because it is very natural and very human to have a strong ego approach to competition. Most people like to win and to look good in the process. But without developing a strong mastery approach, winning will be an infrequent experience, more dependent on luck than on skills. Think about it from a sports point of view. If you were picking teams, who would you want on your team? Someone who cares mainly about looking good, or someone who really wants to be good? Well, you are the first and most important member of your trading team. So are you really good, or do you just try to look good?

Here is what legendary Penn State football coach Joe Paterno has to say on this same subject:

> *Many coaches think of success and excellence as though they are the same. They're not. Success is perishable and often outside our control. In contrast, excellence is something that's lasting, dependable, and largely within a person's control. In sport, in business, in politics, we all know people who are very successful and try to keep other people down. But people who truly excel do not resent excellence in others. People who shoot only for success, however, always feel threatened by other people's success. Success is measured by what other people think; by whether they ask for autographs, buy tickets, stand up to applaud and cheer. Excellence is best measured by the achievers.*

Both an ego and a mastery focus can exist within the same person. You can care about what others think of you and also have a strong desire to be excellent at what you do. But our assumption is that an ego approach comes naturally, whereas a mastery approach takes work and practice. Throughout this book we will be emphasizing a mastery approach to trading. Here is our simple goal: we want you to reach your potential as an online trading athlete. That means that you must keep asking yourself, what can I do to improve as a trader? Why do I want to keep working hard at this? Do I really want to be good at what I do? If you can develop a greater commitment to this mastery approach to trading, we can guarantee that you will enjoy your trading more and achieve at a higher level.

A LOOK AT THE EGO AND MASTERY APPROACH: RAY AND THE DISCUS

My work with Ray is an excellent demonstration of the changes that can occur in moving from an ego to a mastery approach to sport. Ray came to me frustrated because he felt he had the talent to compete with the best throwers in the nation but his results did not back up his confidence. He struck me as a wonderful athlete, with most of the tools to be successful, but his anxiety was holding him back.

When I asked Ray what his goals were, they were focused almost entirely on lots of hard work and physical practice. I asked him if he had any mental goals, but he was puzzled by what I meant. I explained that in my experience, the hardest thing about the Olympics is not the physical demands of the sport, but the emotional pressures that an athlete feels. I explained that it is possible to prepare for these emotional stresses by setting mental training goals. Ray was interested and wanted to learn more. We agreed to work together on some mental training.

One of the hardest things for Ray to do was concentrate at a big meet. He complained that he always felt distracted and unfocused, and admitted that he was somewhat intimidated by the better throwers and their reputations. I asked whether he practiced concentration during workouts, but interestingly, his practices were often unfocused, too. He worked during the day at a shoe store, and would rush to practice to try and get as many throws in as he could. He was often angry with himself during workouts for not throwing as well as he should.

My "diagnosis" of Ray was that he had a strong ego approach, but his mastery approach was weak. He was constantly comparing himself to the best throwers, with the result that he felt inferior to them and thus lacked confidence. In addition, he was putting in lots of practice time, but much of it was not quality practice time, so he was not getting the most out of it. He did not really know how to be the best thrower he could be. I wanted to help Ray develop more confidence by lessening his comparisons to other throwers and by focusing more on what he needed to do to improve.

Ray knew I had helped several of his friends, so he was willing to try my first suggestion, which was to take some time before every practice to sit down, take some deep breaths, and think about what he wanted to accomplish that day. What were his practice goals? What aspects of his technique did he want to work on? How was he going to improve his concentration during the workout?

For example, when we first began to work together, Ray was working on his tempo during throws. He wanted to feel more in rhythm and more in control, and he wanted to "explode" into his release. I asked him to imagine a great throw in his mind before each practice, to really focus on feeling a smooth rhythm and tempo. I also encouraged him to do some deep breathing and to relax right before each throw, to see if this would help him concentrate.

(continued)

Ray was dubious at first, because he was actually doing less work in practice by spending the first 15 minutes "not doing very much but huffing and puffing," as he described it. But to his surprise, he found that he was soon throwing farther, more consistently, than he had ever done before. Each week brought a new practice personal record. He was very excited about his next big meet, and could not wait to show everyone how well he was throwing. But to his consternation, he showed up for the competition and threw poorly; none of his throws approached what he was routinely doing in practice.

Ray was very unhappy the next time we met, and complained that he was not making any progress. I reminded him of how much he had accomplished at his workouts, and suggested that now it was time to bring the same approach to competition. I suggested that he create some time for himself before the next meet to do the same routine he did at workouts—relax, breath deeply, visualize some excellent throws, and go over his goals for the meet. Once again he was full of anticipation of his next competition, and once again he was disappointed because he threw poorly.

When we discussed Ray's goals at our next meeting, he told me that his main goal was to beat his rival, Anthony, and to show some of his other friends how far he was throwing. I went over the basics of the differences between an ego and a mastery approach with Ray and asked him to tell me into which category his goals fell. He said they were ego goals because he was comparing himself to others. I agreed. "Ray," I explained, "as long as you keep comparing yourself with these other guys, you won't have 100 percent concentration to focus on yourself. If you throw really, really, far, does it matter how far Anthony throws?" "No," agreed Ray, "if I throw as well as I can I believe I'll win. But I don't think Anthony respects me. He doesn't think I'm a very good thrower. I want to show him."

After some discussion I convinced Ray to try something different at the next meet. He was to go up to Anthony and compliment him, and then ask him for some advice on a small technical detail of his swing. I wanted Ray to start thinking of Anthony as a potential friend. Ray was also going to set some mental goals for the competition, to focus 100 percent on each throw, to focus on his rhythm and tempo, and to relax and concentrate before each throw. Sure enough, at his next meet, Ray set a new competition personal record. At the meet after that, he won the meet and had the best throw of the year nationally. Not only that, he was surprised to find Anthony was not the hostile, critical enemy he had imagined, but a nice guy who was as much into throwing as Ray was.

Ray went from strength to strength, and a year after we started working together he won the national championship. Of course, most of the credit goes to the tremendous hard work that Ray put in. But I also believe that a turning point occurred when Ray began to learn some mental skills for throwing, and learned to develop a better mastery approach to go along with his natural ego approach to competition.

What we know, and what you will discover, is that the same sport psychology approaches Ray used to achieve excellence will make you a better trader. Think about it, was Ray's situation any different than that of an online trader who wants to find out how much money he made compared to another trader? Such a trader often considers himself a success if he made more and a failure if he made less. This sounds like the same motivational issues occurring in different environments.

Our entire book is filled with simple sport psychology strategies for the online trading athlete, and we have provided many examples to show you how the traders we have worked with have used these strategies to increase their online trading success. All we ask of you is that you consider putting these approaches into your trading game plan so that you can reach your potential as an online trading athlete.

THE RULES OF TRADING

One of our clients, Bryan, developed a set of rules that he used to put some discipline into his trading day. By taking this mastery approach to trading, he was able to concentrate and focus during his trading day. Here is the actual list of eight rules that Bryan used to become a better online trading athlete. These rules worked for him, but as you work your way through this book you will develop your own rules to trade by.

AN ONLINE TRADING ATHLETE'S RULES

1. Read my mission statement every trading day
2. Focus before I sit and begin trading (tell myself it is "game time")
3. Clear my stadium (trading area) of distractions
4. Trade quick, trade confident
5. Three bad trades in a row, take a 10–15 minute break

6. Take a break every 90 to 120 minutes to stay mentally focused
7. If I am going to eat lunch, eat; if I am going to trade, trade
8. If I lose focus, reread mission statement and take three deep breaths

Bryan Taylor

Bryan believed that his rules were a contract that he had with himself. For this reason, he chose to sign them. Because you are also an online trading athlete, we would recommend that you develop your own set of trading rules as you make your way through the book. To help you out, we have provided some general trading rules in each chapter. These are not trading rules about buying low and selling high (remember we are trading coaches, not financial advisors). Rather, these are rules to remind you of what you need to do to be a winning trader; of what you need to focus on to give 100 percent to your trading day; and of what you must keep in mind to achieve excellence as an online trading athlete.

We will come back to these trading rules at the end of the book, and encourage you to sign your own set of rules and make them binding because if you develop a mastery approach to trading and stick to it, you will be around to win all the batting titles your shelf can hold. However, move away from these rules and you might find yourself watching the game from the stands or on television with a lot less in your bank account.

Add your motivation and enthusiasm to our sport psychology strategies, and we believe you have an unbeatable formula for long-term trading success. Take a page out of the handbooks of the great coaches and remember that there are many things that are outside your control—the actions of others, the market, the economy, and the decisions made by companies and their shareholders. You must ignore these things and concentrate on those things you can control. Just as all-stars like Ken Griffey, Jr. and Randy Johnson do not waste time worrying about things outside their control such as umpire calls and crowd noise, you must forget about external distractions and focus your attention on what you can control: your own thoughts and your focus of attention. With your new mission statement and your commitment to becoming a masterful trader, you are now ready to tackle even bigger challenges in the world of online trading. Let us move on to the next important topic, the skill of goal setting.

> *The formula for a good coach: 90 percent talent . . . 90 percent discipline . . . 90 percent work. He must never be satisfied with what he does. It is never as good as it can be done. Always dream and shoot higher than you know you can do. Don't bother just to be better than your contemporaries or predecessors. Try to be better than yourself.*
>
> —William Faulkner

THE MENTAL KEYS TO BECOMING A MASTERFUL ONLINE TRADING ATHLETE

- Start with understanding your motivation
    - The personal trading mission statement
    - Internal versus external motivation

- Long-term success comes from inner motivation
    - The difference between mastery trading and ego trading

- Develop your own rules of trading

CHAPTER TWO

SETTING AND ACHIEVING YOUR GOALS

Glenn is a trader from Chicago who has some clear goals for the coming year. He wants to make at least as much money as he did last year (which was approximately $150,000), he wants to learn more about momentum trading so he can make the transition from a position trader, and he wants to buy a new Range Rover. The big question for Glenn is, does he know how to make his goals really happen? He has had his heart set on that Range Rover for three years, and it has not happened yet. What is going to make this year different?

We all have dreams and hopes, things we would like to see happen if everything goes well. But a goal is not just a pipe dream. It is an objective. It is something we work hard toward. Once we start setting goals, we are serious about becoming successful online trading athletes. The best athletes have goals for every workout, for every practice, for every game. What can we learn from them about how to make our goals a reality? Let us start with an exercise in goal setting.

21

MY TRADING GOALS

Think about three goals you have for the coming year. Choose one goal in each of the following areas:

Financial: What financial goals do you have for the coming year?
Skills: What new skills do you wish to develop, what old skills do you wish to improve?
Learning: What is something you wish to learn about in the coming year?

Write down these three goals:
My *financial* goal for the next year is:

_____

My *skills* goal for the next year is:

_____

My *learning* goal for the next year is:

_____

Keep these goals in mind as you read on. We will return to them in a minute.

EFFECTIVE GOALS

Have you ever set a goal and not reached it? Perhaps a New Year's Resolution to lose 20 pounds by April that was hopeless by February? Very often we blame ourselves for failure to meet our goals. "I didn't have the willpower," complains one person, or "I was just too weak to stick to it," says another. But here is another way to think about it. Sometimes the goals we set are the reason for our failure. Sport psychologists have found that some goals help us move forward and achieve concrete results. Other types of goals actually seem to weigh us down and trip us up. An effective goal is one that helps us stay motivated, focused, and excited.

Sport psychology researchers have found that effective goals share certain common characteristics. Athletes who have goals with these characteristics tend to be successful. Those athletes who do not use these types of goals experience more disappointment. Let us take a look at these six fundamental traits of effective goals. They are:

1. Achievable
2. Strategic
3. Measurable
4. Controllable
5. Flexible
6. Positive

ACHIEVABLE GOALS

Glenn wants to earn at least $150,000 in the coming year. He has good reasons for this goal. He needs that much income to support his family, help pay for their house, save a little for retirement, and, of course pay for his Range Rover. Is the goal achievable? It is because Glenn knows he was able to make that amount last year. So, there is no reason to suggest that he cannot do it again.

Are you capable of reaching your goals in a timely manner? If you set a goal that is unrealistic, you are setting yourself up for failure. A new trader who sets the goal of making $20,000 in the first month of trading may be setting himself up for major disappointment. Is it possible for a new trader to accomplish this goal? Well, probably somewhere in the online trading world a trader has done this in their first month, but I think we would all agree that this would be the exception and not the norm. How do you tell if a goal is achievable? Experience is the best indicator. But if you do not have experience in that area, research is also a good way to determine what makes a goal realistic. What have other traders like you done? What is the average income of beginning traders? How long has it taken other people to reach the same or similar goal? Setting effective goals requires that you start to do your homework. You do not write down what you hope will happen. You write down what you truly believe is going to happen.

Goals also need to be customized to the individual. What might be realistic for a veteran trader most likely is not realistic for a rookie. Five years ago, Glenn was only making $20,000 a year from trading as a hobby. If he had decided to try to make $150,000 the next year by suddenly trading full-time, how successful do you think he would have been?

STRATEGIC GOALS

Goals are useless if you do not have a plan for reaching them. Becoming a successful trader means that you will develop a clear strategy for achieving your goals. The best strategy is to work backwards from your long-term goals, setting weekly and daily goals that will keep you moving toward your long-term objectives. Setting daily and weekly goals helps increase your productivity and effectiveness. These short-term goals show you the way to reach your long-term objectives, and they serve as measures of the progress you are making toward them.

When a basketball player is asked, "What are your goals for this season?" the response is usually along the lines of "To win the championship," or "Help my team in whatever way possible," or "To average 20 points per game." An online trading athlete might identify his or her goals as "To make a living trading" or "Limit my losers and let my winners run." While these are all great goals to have, the problem is they are missing one key ingredient. *How* are you going to achieve this? That is where strategic goal setting comes in.

Outcome goals are the end result or what we would like to accomplish. Strategic goals are what we are going to do to achieve it. Strategic goals describe and outline the process we are going to go through to achieve our end result or outcome goal.

One way that we help competitive athletes and online trading athletes understand the difference between outcome and strategic goals is to draw a picture of a building and tell them to imagine they are standing on the ground and that their goal is to get to the top of the building. We then ask them if this is an outcome or strategic goal. Once they see it as an outcome (end result) goal, we then ask them how they are going to achieve this goal and reach the top of the building. Some of the responses that we have received over the years have been creative and colorful, however, the most common ones include using a staircase, elevator, or climbing. Regardless of the method, the athletes realize that what they are describing is a strategy or process to reaching their initial outcome goal. After clearly differentiating between outcome and strategic goals, we then stress the importance of being specific when setting goals.

The key to strategic goals is to make them as specific as possible. When writing them down, include days of the week, times, locations, anything that helps you take ownership of the goal.

Competitive athletes use something called goal sheets to help them identify, evaluate, and take ownership of their outcome and process goals. The goal sheet serves as a written contract between the athlete and him or herself. It helps keep the athlete committed and focused on their goals. As an online trading athlete, you can use this same strategy.

Our friend Glenn has a major goal of learning about momentum trading in the coming year. Now he must develop a strategy for reaching that goal. What does he need to do to become a successful momentum trader? Glenn made a list of the steps he needs to take. The list looks something like this:

- Pick a small handful of stocks to watch
- Buy a good introductory guide to momentum trading
- Find someone who is an excellent momentum trader and meet or speak with him or her on a regular basis
- Begin doing some momentum trading, keeping my positions small in the beginning until I gain confidence

Glenn is happy with his strategy. It is reasonable and sound. Now where to begin? He decides that experience is the best teacher, and focuses on identifying someone who is already a good momentum trader. He reasons that such a person might also point him toward useful courses, reading materials, and market sectors.

Glenn's immediate goal is to find a successful momentum trader who would be willing to mentor him. He remembers a friend mentioning someone who might be perfect, and decides to give his friend a call to get the phone number.

Once you have a specific, concrete daily goal—I need to find someone who is a successful momentum trader—it becomes much easier to do. When you say "I want to become a good momentum trader in the next year," it seems much more daunting, and you are less likely to even make the effort. To help you more clearly understand how Glenn was able to set up his goal, we have included a sample of his goal sheet (see Figure B).

In a study to measure the effectiveness of short-term goals, sport psychologists asked people who were doing weight-training to set different types of goals. They found that people who set long-range weight training goals plus

FIGURE B   GLENN'S EFFECTIVE GOAL SETTING SHEET

Outcome Goal
My Goal is to

> learn how to momentum trade and make at least $150,000 so I can support my family, save for retirement, and buy a new Range Rover

Is it:	yes	no	why?
Achievable?	✔		b/c I am a quick learner and have been successful
Strategic?	✔		b/c I have a game plan
Measureable?	✔		b/c I can regularly see my P & L statement
Controllable?	✔	✔	b/c I can control myself but not the market
Flexible?	✔		b/c I can go back to position trading if I get stuck
Positive?	✔		b/c I am doing something rather than avoiding it

Strategic Goal

> I want to learn how to become a successful momentum trader

In order to reach this goal, I am going to:

Day	Do what?	At what time?
Monday	follow 2 or 3 stocks, then speak with Dana, my new mentor	before 10:30 am
Tuesday	start reading the new trading book I bought	7 pm to 8 pm
Wednesday	speak with Dana about the market	3 pm to 3:30 pm
Thursday	make 4 small trades to get my feet wet	before 10 am
Friday	speak with Dana about my trades	3 pm to 3:30 pm
Saturday	continue to read book	when I wake up
Sunday	go over my weekly goals for next week	after dinner

some intermediate, stepping-stone goals did much better than people who were just asked to do their best. However, people who set only long-range goals did not do better than the weight-trainers who were asked to do their best.

STEPPING STONES

Nelson Diebel, 1992 gold medal winner of the 100-meter breaststroke in Barcelona, commented, "I use a lot of goal-setting in my swimming. I tend to make one long-term goal and then make little steps along the way. But it's not vitally important that I make all of the goals along the way as long as I keep moving toward the big goal."

"For example," he continued, "in 1988 I was fifth in the 100-meter breaststroke at the Olympic Trials. But I had only been swimming for a year and a half, so I suddenly realized 'I can *do* this swimming thing!' And I said to myself, 'I want to go the Olympics in 1992.' But just setting out in 1988 and making my goal the Olympics in 1992 was too far off, it was too nebulous a concept."

"So I had to constantly make little goals, what times I wanted and so on. I figured that if I kept moving forward one day I would look up from all these little steps I was taking and all of a sudden my big goal would be there. And it was, easily within reach." Diebel concluded, "So having these little short-term goals, these intermediate goals, helps you mentally prepare and also breaks up the monotony of trying for one big goal for an extended period of time."

Start on your goal today. Try the stepping-stone strategy yourself now. Go back to your goals for this year (see beginning of this chapter) and pick one you have been meaning to tackle.

What is the first step toward achieving this goal? Write it down. If you do not know what the first step is, that is your first goal. Find out! Write that goal down!

Find the time to work on that goal today. Schedule an hour of your day for that goal right now. If you cannot spare an hour, make sure you set aside 30 minutes. If you cannot spare 30 minutes, that goal is not important enough for you. Find a new goal you really want to work on.

Do not be afraid to ask for help when developing a strategy for achieving your goals. The more complicated your long-term goal, the harder it will be to break down into small steps. If you do not know how to move forward in small steps toward your long-term goals, it means you need some help working on your plan for success.

All the great athletes depend greatly on good coaches to help them with their goals, so ask yourself who your coach can be. If a coach is not available, think about working on your goals with some friends. Often, the solution to the plan will be easier to see when there are others helping you with their ideas.

MEASURABLE GOALS

Can your goal be measured? An athlete whose goal is to win the gold medal at the 100-meter sprint at the Olympic Games knows that he must run the race in 10 seconds or less to win. If he currently runs an 11-second 100 meters, he can see if he is making progress by charting his times over the course of the season.

But this measurement of overall progress is not enough. As we saw above, the runner must also strategize how he is going to become faster. This will involve some daily workout sessions in the gym, working on increasing lower body strength, arm strength, and working on plyometrics and speed. The effective athlete can measure how well they are doing by checking off the number of workout sessions, and by measuring the types of workouts done in each session.

Effective goal setting requires that you be able to monitor your progress toward achieving your goal. What is the equivalent of these daily workout goals for the online trading athlete? You must be able to look at the parts of your strategy plan and see if you are doing them. If you are setting effective goals, there are only two possible answers:

Yes, I am doing my daily goals. Good, reward yourself, give yourself a pat on the back, and stick to it.

No, I am not doing my daily goals. Then the question becomes, why not? The answer will be very useful to help you become a better trader. Do you have too little time? Not enough energy? Are the goals too hard? Do you get frustrated and give up? For each of these problems, there are some simple solutions. We will look at the most common problems that arise in reaching goals at the end of this chapter, and give you some concrete suggestions for what to do about them.

Feedback is critical for the success of your goal-setting program. If you can build a consistent feedback loop into your goal-setting program, you will be halfway down the road to success. Feedback serves three very important functions.

First, it tells you how well you are doing so that you can make any necessary changes. Second, feedback increases your confidence. Whenever we get positive feedback, we feel good about ourselves, and this makes us more confident for the future. Third, feedback is motivating. You can measure your progress toward your goals. The closer you get, the harder you will work.

You can get regular feedback in several ways. One way is to set goals that are measurable, such as how often you do something. Suppose your goal is to find out which market research software to use. Well, this can be overwhelming because there are so many choices out there, but if you set as your strategic goal learning about two different ones every day for a week, then you can easily keep track of your progress and reach your goal.

Another important factor in becoming a good goal setter is to learn to set goals that are really under your control. We take a look at this important step in the next section.

CONTROLLABLE GOALS

Do you have complete control over whether you will accomplish your goals? A hitter who has set a goal to hit .300 this season has set himself up for failure. Why? Let us take a closer look at it.

Is hitting .300 achievable? Sure, especially if the batter hit .350 last year. Is it measurable? Of course, it is a number. Well then, is it controllable? Wait, before you say, "Yes, he is the one hitting," take a minute to think about what really determines whether he gets a hit or not. There is an umpire who calls balls and strikes, there is a pitcher trying to get the batter out, and most importantly, there are eight other players standing on the field trying to get the batter out as well. The truth is that the hitter could make great contact every time he is up to bat, and end up hitting line drives back to the players in the field. The end result would be that the hitter physically performed well, but it was out of his control whether he got a hit and improved his statistics. If this happens consistently throughout the season, the hitter could end up batting .200, thereby falling short of his goal, which appeared to be achievable before the season.

This example is exaggerated, but what commonly happens to athletes is that they set goals that are out of their control and when they start to fall short of their expectations, they see their lack of performance as a personal failure on their part. They then begin to try harder or make mechanical adjustments to their swing, and before long, they end up in a performance slump. So the batter who was hitting line drives every time now feels as if he could not hit water if he fell out of a boat. And all of this occurred because he viewed his low batting average as an indication of poor performance rather than an inevitable part of factors in the game that were out of his control.

For online trading athletes, the perspective is the same. As a trader, you are the hitter, the stock you are trading is the pitcher, and the market is the team on the field. Making a quality trade (hitting line drives) does not always mean that you will have a profitable trade (hit). Because once you make contact (hit the enter button to make the trade), it is out of your control what happens next. Traders who fall into performance slumps begin to doubt their trading style because of the financial outcome of the trade rather than viewing the situation as "I made a quality decision, there were simply some factors that were out of my control." In the trading world, this often is referred to as losing money on a good trade. And believe us, there is such a thing. Therefore, it is very important for you, as a trader, to focus on the goals you can control—not the performance of the market, which is beyond anyone's control.

Factors under your control are numerous. They include:

- The amount of research you do on a trade or a stock
- Sticking to stocks or sectors you know well
- Buying and selling within your game plan rather than based on a rumor you heard in the bathroom
- Staying within your trading limits

If you focus on what you can control, you can remain confident in your performance even when you encounter the inevitable setbacks that come with being an online trading athlete. Just as the baseball player who goes 0-for-4 in one game can refocus on his solid swing and step up to the plate the next day with his confidence intact, you can stay calm and focused even if you have several unprofitable trading sessions in a row. If the baseball player who stays focused and confident can sidestep what normally would have been the beginning of a performance slump then you too can avoid trading slumps, and a lot of grief and misery, by doing the same.

FLEXIBLE GOALS

Flexibility, which is the fifth characteristic of effective goal setting that we have examined, looks at the question, "Are you willing to adjust your goals to achieve success?" Achieving success is, for the most part, about confidence and we will talk more in depth about confidence later in this book. However, being flexible with your goals is one way to maintain your confidence levels as an online trading athlete. If you have set a goal to make 50 quality trades per day but find that during the summer the market seems to slow down, you have two choices. You can continue to make the 50 trades per day, but feel yourself forcing some trades or making nonquality trades, or you can be flexible and adjust your initial goal of making 50 trades to making 20 quality trades per day until the market picks up after the summer. In the first choice, you will reach your daily goal but at the expense of your confidence level and some money, because you will most likely be pressing and making some nonquality trades. In the second choice, you are reevaluating the situation and adjusting your goals to accommodate the environment, thereby reaching your daily goal along with maintaining or increasing, not only your level of confidence, but also your trading account.

POSITIVE GOALS

When you write down your strategic goals, make them as precise and clear as possible. State them in the first person whenever you can, for example "I will . . ." This will help you feel like it is your goal. Say, "I will go online on Saturday morning to begin to research which trading analysis software packages are out there" instead of, "My research will be finished on Saturday."

Don't say don't. It is also important to make your goals positive. It is human nature to concentrate on the last thing you were told. So if a coach tells a young running back "Don't fumble," the running back is more likely to think about fumbling. In contrast, the suggestion, "Keep the ball tucked into your chest," is helpful. It is good specific advice that gives the running back something concrete on which to focus.

The trader who sets a goal such as, "I won't lose money in the coming month" is making the same mistake. Instead of focusing on a positive goal, he is focusing on a potential mistake. This typically causes high levels of anxiety and actually hurts performance levels. It is not helpful to focus attention on a problem without providing a solution.

Instead of using "Don't" goals or "We will *not* . . ." goals, think of a possible solution to the target problem. Base the goal on this solution. For example, if a trader wants to avoid a losing month, it might be best if he trades well within his limits, sticks to stocks he knows best, and is disciplined about executing his trades according to his timetable. All these goals can be stated positively and promote confidence rather than anxiety.

We know that thinking negative goals is a tough habit to break. So how about we step onto the driving range and take some practice swings to get rid of that slice. Take a minute or two to practice reframing your goals so they become assets to your game rather than obstacles in your performance.

Reword each negative goal to create a positive one (we did the first two for you to get you on track).

Old Goal

To not have any more than 10 losing trades each day

New Goal

To make 10 quality trades each day

Old Goal

To not hesitate when getting out of a bad or losing trade

New Goal

To stick to my game plan, cut my losses, and move on

Old Goal

To stop trading so many sectors

New Goal

_____

Old Goal

To not trade when the market is slow

New Goal

_____

Old Goal

To stop taking out small bids and offers just to get in the market

New Goal

_____

So, how is that swing coming? Getting the hang of it? Great, now let us move on and end our chapter on goals by taking a minute or two to look at exactly why goals work.

WHY DO GOALS WORK?

Why are goals so powerful? What is it about writing down a goal that helps us achieve at a much higher level? Here are some final thoughts on why goals work. If you understand how powerful goals can be, hopefully we can convince you to make goal setting a daily part of your trading life.

If you don't know where you're going, you probably won't end up there.

—Yogi Berra

Begin with the end in mind.

—Stephen Covey

Effective goals influence our performance in the following ways.

- We increase the amount of time we spend on the goal.
- We increase the effort we put into achieving the goal.
- We persist in the face of setbacks.
- We are more focused on our objective.
- We prioritize more clearly when we have goals.
- We develop strategies to achieve our goals.

The bottom line is that without effective goals, you may never be able to reach your potential as online trading athlete.

Remember, learning how to use effective goals is a process that is going to take some time so take a deep breath, keep your head up and your shoulders back as we move to our next chapter and talk about confidence.

A variety of goal-setting worksheets for you to use are provided in Appendix A, pages 236–246.

SETTING AND ACHIEVING YOUR GOALS

- The principles of effective goals
    - Achievable
    - Strategic
    - Measurable
    - Controllable
    - Flexible
    - Positive

- Effective goals influence our performance in the following ways
    - We increase the amount of time we spend on the goal
    - We increase the effort we put out in the goal
    - We persist in the face of setbacks
    - We are more focused on our objective
    - We prioritize more clearly when we have goals
    - We develop strategies to achieve our goals

CHAPTER THREE

CONFIDENCE: THE FOUNDATION OF SUCCESS

Vince Carter makes a thunderous over-the-head dunk; Jason Kidd makes an amazing no-look behind-the-back pass to a wide-open scorer; Marcus Camby soars through the air to swat away an attempted basket. If you watch pro sports, you will soon see examples of athletes playing "in the zone," playing with a grace and ease that results from years of hard work and practice. When an athlete is in the zone for an extended period, they feel they cannot miss, that they cannot be guarded, and that they will win no matter what. This same feeling of tremendous confidence can also occur for traders. Traders who talk about feeling "in the zone" say that on those days, everything they touch turns to gold. They feel they can do no wrong. They are trading in an effortless, almost instinctual way. It is as if they have a perfect instinct for what the market and their sector is about to do.

Being in the zone is the ultimate state of confidence. Here are some sport-specific examples of playing in the zone.

- *Baseball:* The hitter sees everything in slow motion and the ball seems to be the size of a beach ball.
- *Basketball:* The player feels as if he or she is on cruise control moving down the court and the basket seems to be a vacuum cleaner sucking in every shot.
- *Golf:* The golfer rips that four iron and watches the ball clear the water and land pin-high three feet from the cup.
- *Football:* The quarterback gets that mystical feeling that he has built-in radar, reading the defense and targeting his open receivers.

For trading athletes, the zone is those rare and precious moments when they feel they have a sixth sense that allows them to collect profits on a stock's daily volatility. Going long and buying it on the way up and then dumping it out as the market begins to turn, then without hesitation, they react—shorting it on the way down and cleaning up at the bottom. Now that is trading "in the zone"!

This chapter is about confidence, the feeling that gives you the courage to face the market every day, and to back your methods, your systems, and your instincts. There is no success without confidence. Only a confident trader can commit hundreds of thousands of dollars to a trade and ride it out to the best outcome. A trader without confidence is crippled. They will miss golden opportunities by hesitating when all the signs tell them to react, they will freeze up when their trade goes against them causing them to take heavy, unnecessary losses, and they will nervously close out a position before realizing its full potential. In this chapter, we show you how to become—and stay—confident in all trading situations, even when the market has been going against you.

CONFUSING CONFIDENCE WITH DISCIPLINE

Probably the most important lesson you can learn from this book is the following:

Becoming a successful online trading athlete is not about making money—it is about limiting your losses.

Stop and think about that for a second. Does it make any sense? What we are saying is that in the trading game, just like going long or short are technically the same just different directions, making money or limiting losses are the same. In other words, the less money you lose, the more money you will be able to clear as profit. Understand? We know it is an unusual way to think about the trading game, but it really is the key to becoming a successful trader.

After all, how many times have you or another trader you know had more winning trades than losing trades in a given day but still ended up with less money in the account after the closing bell rings? Believe us, it is extremely common, especially among rookie traders. Let us tell you about a trader we recently worked with who was going through this exact problem. In order to protect his identity, we are going to call this trader Paul.

Paul contacted our firm one day saying that he was having confidence problems. He had been trading for two years and still had not been able to turn a decent profit. As a result, his available funds had dwindled and he was now limited to trading very small sizes. In addition, he told us that if his first couple of trades were losers, he had to stop trading for the day because he would not have enough capital for the next day. After talking with Paul for about 30 minutes, it became clear that he was having confidence problems but that these problems were stemming from his trading style. In other words, Paul had the skills it took to be successful, he was simply not disciplined enough to trust himself and stick with them.

Thinking that there was most likely a pattern to his trading cycle, we asked Paul if he kept a trading log. He did, so we proceeded to talk about it. What we noticed, with Paul's help, was that his winners were no more than a half point at a time while his losers were two, three, or even four points at time. When we asked him what he thought about this, he said that when a stock went his way, he would become euphoric and immediately close out the position to lock in his profit. However, when a trade went against him, he would ruminate over it and try to ride it out. Eventually he would be so deep in the hole that he gave himself no choice but to liquidate at a significant loss. In addition, we found that many of his "big losers" were trades that he entered into when the market was slow (e.g., during lunch hours). When we asked him why he thought he did this, he responded by saying, "I don't know why, I guess it's because I get bored when nothing is going on."

You see, what Paul identified as a confidence issue was really a discipline issue. Sure his confidence had shriveled to nothing as a result of repeatedly taking heavy losses, but to get himself back on track, he needed to understand that the key to becoming a successful trader was not making money but rather limiting his losses.

So, what did we suggest that Paul do to help him get back into the game? Well, we focused on two things. The first was to encourage him to pick a two-hour block of time in the day to trade, either early morning or afternoon. This would provide some structure to his trading style. And the second was to encourage him to begin each trade with the end in mind by setting specific limits to his trading before he opened a position. In other words, if Paul was not disciplined enough on his own to get out of a bad trade, then we encouraged him to use sell or buy stops (depending on whether he was long or short) to ensure that his position would close out before it ballooned into a huge loser. We know some of you veteran traders are thinking that using stop orders does not give a position enough room to breath, but remember, our goal was to help Paul develop discipline.

Admittedly, Paul was reluctant to try this new approach because he felt as if he was going back to the basics. This was, of course, a perfectly natural reaction of any trader who had been in the game for a decent amount of time. But once he realized that his lack of success was because of a lack of discipline not confidence, he was able to challenge himself to restructure his trading style and learn the skill of discipline. It took some time and a great deal of patience, but Paul was eventually able to build up his account and continue his career as an online trading athlete by learning how to make a profit through limiting his losses.

As Paul's example shows, oftentimes the obstacles that traders face are not as obvious as they appear. The next section of this chapter deals with how you can establish your confidence by simply understanding the trading game in its most basic form.

SOMETIMES YOU WIN, SOMETIMES YOU LOSE, SOMETIMES IT RAINS

Let us put trading in perspective. No matter what the scenario, on any given day only three things can happen to market prices.

1. They can go *up*
2. They can go *down*
3. They can remain *unchanged*

There is a great line in the movie *Bull Durham* where the coach of the minor league Durham Bulls team calls all of the players in for a meeting. The team has been going through a bad slump, everyone's confidence is down in the dumps and he is searching for some way to motivate his players back into action. Creatively, he decides to simplify the game of baseball for them. The coach's words of wisdom went something like this: "Baseball is a simple game. You see the ball, you hit the ball, you catch the ball, and you throw the ball. Sometimes you win, sometimes you lose, and sometimes it rains."

The message that the coach was trying to convey was that oftentimes, the best way to view a situation is to break it down to its simplest form. This strategy can help you locate your confidence when you have fallen off track. In the trading game, just as in baseball, sometimes you win (make money), sometimes you lose (lose money), and sometimes it rains (break even). Remember, the market either goes up, goes down, or remains unchanged. Any questions? Now let us look at the most difficult part of any competitive situation and the most common confidence killer—failure.

PLAYING TO WIN

One of the chains that holds many traders back from a successful career in trading is the fear of failure. This affects many areas of life. No one likes to fail, and the fear of how stupid we might look, or concern about what others might think of us should we fail stops many of us from competing.

As sport psychologists, this fear of failure is something we deal with constantly. It can ruin a promising career in sports before it even gets off the ground because a sports career, similar to a trading career, is built on a foundation of failure. Only through failure can an athlete learn the vital lessons necessary to eventually become a consistent winner. If you are afraid to compete because you are afraid to fail, you are doomed to your current level, with no hope of improvement. The risk of competition also carries with it the reward of growth.

We find that many athletes begin to perform at a higher level when they change their attitude toward competition. You can also change your attitude and we believe that you will also perform at a higher level when you do so. A good place to start is to examine your attitude toward losing. Does the thought of being a loser scare you? How would you feel if we called you a loser right now?

If you are like many young athletes, the label "loser" is one you will do anything to avoid. We have allowed it to become a scary label, a word that is such an insult that it can cause fights between friends. Yet being a loser is what competition is all about. There are no great winners without great losers, and very few winners are not losers first. Why should we be afraid of something that can often be a symbol of honor and pride?

Part of the reason is that many of us believe what we read in the sports pages every day. Nowhere is more garbage written about sports by people who know nothing about athletes than in the sports section of daily newspapers. One of the favorite quotes of these "sports journalists" is that "nobody remembers second place." They make it sound as if only by winning a competition can you succeed. Losers are consigned to the trash heap of history.

We can prove just how wrong this saying is by asking you to name the greatest Super Bowl you have ever seen. If you are a bit older, you might name the 1979 Super Bowl between the Steelers and the Cowboys, which Pittsburgh won by a score of 35–31. If you are younger, you might cite the thrilling "wide right" game of 1991, when the New York Giants beat the Buffalo Bills, 20–19, or the back-and-forth tussle between Brett Favre's Packers and John Elway's Broncos in the 1998 Super Bowl, when Denver hung on for a 31–24 victory; or perhaps the great 2000 game between the Tennessee Titans and the St. Louis Rams, won by Kurt Warner's Rams, 24–17.

What do all these great games have in common? Did you name only the winner when you picked your greatest game ever? No! *Both* teams are remembered in a great contest, and this is always true in sports. It takes a really great opponent to make a really great champion. Each of the teams mentioned above—the Cowboys, Bills, Packers, and Titans—were losers according to the sports journalists, but to fans they were the reason for an exciting contest that was greatly enjoyed, and these "losers" will be remembered long after many winners of blow-out games are forgotten.

Successful competitive athletes and trading athletes are both experts at dealing with failure. They are able to recognize when their timing is off and they take the time to step away and refocus. They also know that regardless of the score that they are winners. Greg Norman said it best after going through a tough loss on pro tour "I am a winner. I just didn't win today." The following story about one of the greatest tennis rivalries in history may help to illustrate this point.

NOBODY REMEMBERS SECOND PLACE

Perhaps one of the greatest tennis contests ever was the 1980 Wimbledon men's final between Bjorn Borg and the young John McEnroe. Borg was vying for his fifth straight championship—an amazing feat—and McEnroe was trying for his first. The tennis prowess they displayed was remarkable. Borg held a two sets to one lead entering the fourth set, which proved to be the ultimate in drama. Neither player could break through the other, and so the set went to a tiebreaker, requiring one of them to reach seven points and lead by two. It did not happen. First Borg would have a match point, then McEnroe a set point, but neither could clinch. Whoever was staring disaster in the face would simply come up with an astonishing winner to tie the game again. The tension became extraordinary. They were tied at 10–10, 12–12, 16–16, and finally, with the crowd hanging on every point, McEnroe won the set 20–18 in the tiebreaker. Even more remarkably, Borg then gathered himself and fought back from what must have been crushing disappointment to win the grueling fifth set, 8–6, and claim his fifth Wimbledon Championship. The crowd went wild and history was made.

Did McEnroe's performance mark him as a loser? When you think about it, if you make your best effort and lose, there is nothing to be ashamed of or scared of in competition. McEnroe's loss was more heroic than many wins, and with the right attitude you can approach your defeats in the same way. There is always another day. John McEnroe bounced back from his 1980 loss to defeat Borg in the Wimbledon final the very next year, and went on to earn three Wimbledon championships.

So are you afraid of losing? Just remember that everyone remembers second place—if it was a good fight.

DEALING WITH FAILURE

As great athletes will tell you, success is more often about overcoming failure than it is about winning because failure is a natural part of life. No one has ever received a grade of 100 percent on every test they have ever taken. No one has ever won every game they have ever played, and most definitely, there has never been a trader whose every trade turned out to be a winner. With this in mind, let us take another look at the game of baseball to see how important confidence is in making a successful athlete.

A baseball player who fails 7 out of 10 times is considered an all-star. Think about that for a moment. This means that you only have to be successful 3 out of 10 times to be considered one of baseball's hitting elite. Even the highest season batting average of all time belonged to a player who failed 6 out of 10 times. That is because a baseball player who gets a hit 4 times out of every 10 at-bats but who makes an out the other six times ends up with a batting average of .400. The few times in recent history when a player approached the end of the season with a chance to be hitting .400, the media went crazy because the last time it was done over an entire season was by Ted Williams in 1941. This example clearly illustrates that even the most successful athletes have to deal constantly with failure. So how do top athletes deal with failure? Athletes who focus on their mistakes and worry about their lack of performance will soon be out of the game. However, a player who views failures as part of the game, as something from which to learn, and who remains confident despite setbacks is one who will have a successful career. The same is true for trading athletes.

Understanding the reality behind success and failure can help you become a confident trading athlete. Losing Wimbledon in 1980 did not prevent John McEnroe from achieving future success, and if you want to become an all-star trading athlete, you should not let it deter you either.

Of course you are going to experience setbacks and question your abilities every now and then. That is normal. Sometimes you may even have the feeling that your confidence seemed to vanish into thin air for no apparent reason. Or you might even say to yourself, "I used to have it. Where did it go? How do I find it?" If you have experienced this before, do not panic! The good news is, you are not alone and we can help you. The bad news is, you are probably going to experience this emotion again sometime in your career. But hopefully the ideas that we talk about in the next section will help limit the amount of time you spend searching for your confidence the next time you feel you "can't find it."

FIGHTING SLUMPS

What is confidence? Confidence is the feeling or belief that you know you are going to get the job done. It is a frame of mind, an attitude, a perspective. It is something you can control (see Chapter 2). Competitive athletes and trading athletes usually experience a loss of confidence when they fail to meet their performance expectations. An athlete who loses confidence is either experiencing a performance slump or is about to enter into one. It is difficult to determine which comes first, the slump or the loss of confidence, but one thing is for sure, where there is one, the other is close behind. Both the successful competitive athlete and trading athlete view slumps as a temporary condition rather than a permanent situation.

An example of a baseball player in a slump is when he is hitting 1 for 10 in his last five games. An example of a trader in a slump is when he or she feels as if they are always on

the wrong side of a trade and every trade they make immediately goes the wrong way almost as if the market knows
what they are thinking.

Dan, a young trader in his mid-20s, had been trading the
NASDAQ for a year and a half. His first couple of months were
a bit inconsistent but he eventually grew into his own and was
a making a great living and feeling on top of the world. While
his college friends were slaving away at investment banking
jobs, pulling 60-hour weeks, he was enjoying the luxury of a
flexible schedule and huge profits. Dan seemed to develop a
knack for the trading game. He had that "golden touch" that
some people seem to be born with and that those who were
not come to resent. Sure, Dan had put in his hours in learning how to trade, but he seemed to adjust quickly to the high-
pressure environment of the trading world, which he attrib-
uted to his experience as a major college football player. He
loved what he did for a living, and he had become extremely
comfortable in his own trading style.

As his confidence grew, so did his position size. Several
months ago, he would think twice before opening a 500-
share position, but now he was throwing around thousands
of shares at a time. To Dan, trading seemed effortless and
magical. He truly believed that this was what he was born to
do. He thrived on the rush of making a big trade and then
monitoring his position until he was able to liquidate it for
a huge profit. It was as if trading had filled the excitement
of competition that he missed from his game days in college.
Life could not get any better for this guy. When the market
would dip, it always seemed like he was on the right side of
the trade. When stocks would have gap openings, he always
seemed to be long on some shares. This went on for nearly
a year and despite taking large sums of money out to "live
the good life" he had managed to build up his account to
more money than most people make in 10 years. Then, one
day—he was not sure when—something changed.

Positions he would put on seemed to run away from him. Every time he was long, he would get stuck in a bear fast market and be unable to liquidate his position. By the time he started to suck it up and take the loss, the market would settle down and show some signs of an upswing so he would hold the position despite experiencing that numb feeling all over his body. Of course, the position would not come back to its original level, it just kept slowly dropping until he finally faced reality and had to liquidate. In an effort to change his negative pattern, he began to take some short positions but this only made matters worse. Once he committed to being short, the market would instantly turn on him and show signs of recovery so he would reverse his position to try to ride the momentum but there was nothing there to ride. The market would tank and he would, once again, take a loss on both sides this time.

Dan could not buy a winning trade. Weeks went by where his account did not have a single winner, just a seemingly endless string of losers. To make matters worse, he was convinced that his previous success was just a fluke and that his luck had run out. He honestly felt like the market was reading his mind and knew which way he was going, and therefore, he believed he was stuck in a hopeless situation. For a trader who had been on such a high for so long, he was now smack in the middle of a slump, feeling depressed with no idea of how to recover.

Desperate to make a comeback, Dan gathered all of his emotional strength, picked himself up off the ground, brushed himself off, and dug deep inside to gather the courage he needed to try to get back in the market. But it was no use. Bad trades were turning into worse trades and each time he got knocked down, it took him longer to get back up until he finally threw in the towel and was forced into early retirement from the trading game.

What can Dan's unfortunate story teach us about how to deal with slumps? For the most part, competitive athletes and trading athletes such as Dan view slumps as negative situations and something to avoid at all costs. Perhaps if Dan was able to view his slump as an inevitable and necessary part of achieving performance excellence, he would still be around trading the market today. With this in mind, here are six ways of looking at a slump that can not only help you overcome it but also turn it into an invaluable learning experience.

1. Realize and believe that the performance slump is just a temporary condition rather than a permanent situation.
2. Take time to examine the events that led up to the slump. Identify when, how, and why it started. Learn from this information.
3. View the slump as a recovery period, an opportunity to reevaluate your game plan and strengthen your commitment to the game.
4. Fighting it will only keep you there longer. Tolerate it rather than fight it. Be patient, focused, and ready to break out of it when the opportunity appears. When you fight the slump and try to force yourself out of it, you usually end up burying yourself deeper in it and prolonging it.
5. View the slump as a mental vacation rather than a dreaded nightmare. (Believe us, it works!) This is the power of positive thinking and it will keep your head above water.
6. A performance slump may be inevitable, but how you interpret it is completely within your control. If you think it is the worst thing that can happen to you, you will have a terrible experience while your performance is off. If you see a slump as a temporary setback and an opportunity to gather your focus, a period of lower performance

will be tolerable as you prepare for greater successes to come.

In order to help you maintain this perspective while working your way through performance slumps, here are two additional strategies that are terrific for increasing your confidence: body language and establishing a regular routine.

BODY LANGUAGE

Confidence is often displayed most clearly via an athlete's body language. The way an athlete carries himself or herself sends a powerful message to their inner psyche. The concept behind this power of positive posture is rooted in what is known as a psychosomatic response. In basic terms, the mind and the body are two separate but interactive entities. We use the example of dreams to explain this to both competitive athletes and online trading athletes.

Have you ever had a dream that you were flying or falling or being chased? Most likely you have because these are very common dreams. Take the dream of falling as an example. You might be sleeping and dreaming that you have fallen off of a building and are hurtling helplessly downward through the air. Your legs and arms flail in space. Suddenly, you wake up just before you hit the ground, your heart racing, covered in sweat. Now let us take a second to think about this. Were you really falling? Of course not, you were safe and sound in your comfortable bed; however, your body really believed that you were falling, as shown by your increased heart rate and perspiration. The point is that your mind was able to convince your body that it was experiencing something that was not really happening. Your body did not know any better. It simply believed whatever scenario your mind created for it, and responded physiologically. This is a psychosomatic response.

This can work both ways. In the dream example, your mind fooled your body into thinking it was doing something that it was not. When you are awake, you can use this same approach by having your physiology jumpstart your mind. And that is where the power of body language comes into play.

Using the same psychosomatic principle that applied in the dream scenario, we can use body language to convince our mind that we are alert, confident, and prepared for what lies ahead. Think of your mind as an auditor that is constantly taking inventory of your body.

Here are two scenarios that the mind is likely to uncover while doing its continual inventory sweep:

SCENARIO #1

Findings: Feet are achy, shoulders are slumped over, and posture is bent

Conclusion: My body seems to be negative therefore I must be exhausted

SCENARIO #2

Findings: Head is up, shoulders are back, and posture is straight

Conclusion: My body seems to be positive therefore I must be alert, prepared, and confident

It is important to realize that your body language mirrors how you feel and how you feel is being reinforced by your body language. The bottom line is that it is a circle where both factors continually feed each other (see Figure C).

The good news is that you can learn to use positive body language as a weapon to fight off destructive and negative

FIGURE C   CONFIDENCE MIRROR

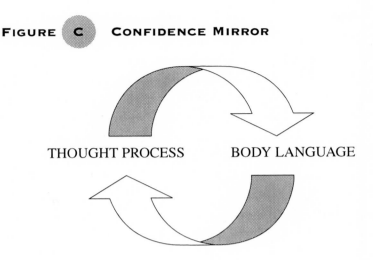

THOUGHT PROCESS   BODY LANGUAGE

thoughts. Just as athletes learn to give their confidence a boost by changing their posture and attitude, you can approach your trading more confidently by following these four simple suggestions:

1. Learn to be aware that when negative thoughts arise, you may be expressing negative body language.
2. Stand up from your chair and take one or two deep cleansing breaths to break the negative thought pattern and regain focus. (See Appendix A, Part I).
3. Lift your head up, put your shoulders back, and assume a tall posture. Then return to your seat maintaining this confident body language.
4. Take one or two final deep cleansing breaths to solidify the positive momentum you have created.

By following these four easy steps you are psychosomatically sending a message to your mind that you are confident, alert, and ready to attack the market with a newfound resilience. Try it out and use this confidence booster as often as necessary during a busy day.

ROUTINES

Have you ever heard the expression, "He's playing in his comfort zone"? Athletes try to create an environment that allows them the greatest opportunity to be successful. This does not mean that they can always guarantee success. It does mean that they can regularly put themselves in a position to be successful. An important method of staying comfortable and relaxed for many athletes is establishing a regular routine. An example of an athlete's routine would include eating a good breakfast on game day, arriving at the competition site in plenty of time to prepare mentally for the game, and rehearsing the team strategy before taking the field. All these little details can add up in terms of making the difference between winning and losing.

Similarly, some of the elements in a successful trading athlete's routine might include checking their favorite news resources before the market opens; making sure to stay properly hydrated and physically alert during a long trading day; establishing the right time when they tell themselves that it is "game time"—time to sit down and trade; when they will take lunch or relaxation breaks; and how many breaks they will take during a day. A solid routine can be thought of as the backbone of a successful trader.

THE WINNING TRADER'S ROUTINE

Shelley is a veteran of the trading game and has been trading for over five years.

"I always wake up at least two hours before the market opens, that way I have time to prepare for the day. I get out of bed, turn on the television, and jump in the shower. Sure there are days when I feel flat or worn out, but I think to myself how much money there is out there just waiting to end up in my account by the time the closing bell rings and that seems to perk me up pretty good.

"After I get dressed, I sit down to eat something, usually a bagel and some juice, and watch CNBC. When I am done, I then get my bottle of water and go to my trading stadium (which is in my spare room). After I sit down, the first thing I do is read my motivation (mission) statement twice—once to myself and then once out loud. The reason I read it twice is because several months ago I read it to myself and then, just for kicks, I read it again out loud and I ended up having one of my best trading days ever so I have been doing it ever since.

"After I am done reading my motivation statement, I do a little inventory, make sure that my desk is clear from distractions, and I do a quick maintenance check (printer, computer resources, software, power plugs, and so on). When I am done with that, I then take 5 to 10 minutes to review my daily/weekly goals and see if I need to make any adjustments. Once everything checks out, I then tell myself that I am capable of achieving my goals. Believe it or not, this is probably one of the most important things that I do in my routine because I occasionally have a discipline and confidence problem and this helps to keep me focused and on track. It is funny, I never thought that by keeping a daily and weekly goals sheet that it would improve my discipline in the market but somehow it does. Maybe it is because I am able to carry over into my trading game the same discipline that I use in keeping a goal sheet. Who knows? But I will tell you this, it works!

"Once I am done with my goal sheet, there are usually about 45 minutes before the market opens. I take this time to go over my game plan for the day. I check my financial sites and any news releases that happened overnight. I find out what reports are being released today in my sectors. I look over some of the charts of the stocks that I follow and I always have an eye on what I call my 'rose garden.'

Basically, this is the sector or stock that I track every once in a while to see if there is any opportunity there, that way if my primary sector slows down or if something starts happening in that other area, then I am ready to go with it. If the rose garden starts to pick up, then I might even trade it regularly, and if that happens, then I keep an eye out for a new rose garden. No matter what, I always have one or two 'roses' waiting on the sidelines. (If there is anything I have learned in my five years of trading online it is that the successful traders are always one step ahead of the game!)

"This whole process takes me about 30 minutes, but I remember when it used to take me hours just to go through all that information. I suppose experience is one of those things in the trading game that you cannot teach someone. Now I am at the point where I don't waste my time with the unnecessary stuff, I just concentrate on what's important. Anyway, by the time I am finished reviewing my game plan and all of these resources, I'll have about 15 minutes before the market opens. So, I go and take a bathroom break (there is nothing worse than being in a position that's moving and having to go to the bathroom) or at least stretch my legs a bit before the market opens. After I am done, I'll get back in my trading stadium and about a minute before the market opens, I'll close my eyes and take three smooth, relaxed breaths and say to myself, 'focus-relax-succeed.'

"I then open my eyes, wait a couple of seconds for the market to open and I am ready to go!"

THE STRUGGLING TRADER'S ROUTINE

Craig is a rookie in the trading game and has been trading for only eight months.

"I usually roll out of bed 15 to 20 minutes before the market opens. I quickly brush my teeth and grab a cup of coffee from the kitchen. I then rush to my room (where my computer is) and I get online to begin trading. Sometimes, I miss the opening but I don't really think it matters because it's easier to get in on a trade when things slow down.

"Once I get online, I like to get in on some chat rooms to find out what people are doing in the market. Some of the tips I get from the chat rooms are pretty good. In fact, I bought some shares yesterday based on a tip from this person in the ##### chat room and he/she said the stock was going to go to the 'moon'. Boy I can't wait, I may even buy some more today. Oh yeah, I also like to watch some television while I am trading. The best part is when they have those experts on the financials giving their stock picks, I get some really great leads from them. I admit I have not made any money just yet, but that's because I'm new at this stuff and I hear it takes a while to catch on.

"This is the best job a guy could have. I trade for a little while and then when I get bored I do some online gaming. A lot of times, I'll put a position around lunchtime and because the market is slow, I'll grab some lunch or talk on the phone or play games. Then when things start to pick up, I can see if my trade was a winner or a loser. If it's a winner, then I get rid of it immediately so I can lock in my profit, but if the trade goes against me then I may even keep it overnight and hope that it will come back the next day.

"I don't think trading is easy but I kind of feel like I am developing a pretty good system. I just need some more time before I get the hang of it and start making some big money."

It is pretty clear how different these two routines are. Shelley is organized, disciplined, motivated, and successful while Craig is disorganized, lazy, poorly motivated, and unsuccessful (and not because he is "new at this stuff"). Shelley has established a successful career as an online trading athlete while we seriously doubt whether Craig will ever "catch on."

Routines are powerful tools. As an online trading athlete, you might think of your routine as your daily checklist to success. Your routine does not have to be exactly like Shelley's, in fact, it should not be. Your job is to find out what works for you and what will help you reach your potential as an online trading athlete. To help you with this, we have some suggestions to help you think of important factors that you might wish to include in your daily routine.

ROUTINE CHECKLIST

The following questions can help you develop a consistent approach to trading. You may not be able to answer all of these questions your first time through. There may be some questions you have not really thought about before. That is fine. The question remains: are you disciplined enough to take some quality time to put together good answers to these questions, so that you can establish a confident, consistent approach to your trading? If you are, then we think you will find it time well spent!

- What surroundings do you like to trade in?
- Do you take the time to create your own championship trading stadium?
- Are there things you can change in your trading stadium (e.g., well-organized desk, better lighting, more comfortable chair) that will help you stay confident and focused?
- When you are taking on a new task that is time consuming, such as working with new software or researching a new market sector, what factors help you stay alert and energized?
- What things can you say to yourself to stay calm and focused?
- What images and mental pictures help you feel confident?

- Do you have regular breaks worked into your daily trading schedule?
- How do you prepare mentally the night before major economic numbers or big earnings reports come out?
- Do you have a "go to" plan that you can tap into if you are caught in a tough market?
- Just before you trade, what is your cue to remind yourself that you are a confident, successful online trading athlete?

If you think carefully about these questions, you will be able to come up with a terrific routine that will put you in the right frame of mind to be a successful trader. Put confidence to work for you, and success will be yours for the taking.

Well, that wraps up confidence. Now it is time to move on to the next chapter where we talk about the difference between a bad trade and a losing trade.

CONFIDENCE: THE FOUNDATION
OF SUCCESS

- Confidence does not equal discipline
- Sometimes you win, sometimes you lose, sometimes it rains
- Confidence
    — Dealing with failure
    — Fighting slumps
- Confidence boosters

    — Body language
    — Routine

CHAPTER FOUR

How Winners Handle Losing

Bad Trades

A successful online trading athlete knows that there is a difference between a bad trade and a losing trade. Just because a trade is not profitable does not mean it is a bad trade. Bad trades are trades that are made without careful consideration and substantial reason. But if you execute a trade for all the right reasons, as part of your strategy, and it still fails, it is not a bad trade, it is just a losing trade. No one can avoid losing trades. They are part of the trading and investment game. But bad trades can and should be avoided. Too many bad trades are the death knell for a successful trading career. Often, online trading athletes who start to make frequent bad trades have strayed from their game plan and begun initiating trades out of frustration or carelessness.

A CAREER-ENDING
BAD TRADE

Mike, a veteran trader, learned a valuable lesson early in his trading career about sticking to his game plan. When he first began trading online, he was at a small trading house. The trader next to him, Bill, was suffering through a streak of losing trades. Bill was not losing a lot of money but he sure was not making any. He was clearly in a performance slump. After a few weeks, Bill was desperate to get himself out of the hole he was in. It is important to note that Bill was not a big trader and always kept his trades under 500 hundred shares. In addition, he was new at online trading and was trying to make a career change from being a discount broker to trading for his own account. One day, Bill finally reached his limit with his performance.

Bill: Mike, I'm struggling.

Mike: Yeah, I know what you mean, it has been choppy all month long.

Bill: Have you been following this stock? I overheard Sharon and Ted talking about how they think it is being targeted for a merger. I've been reading the news releases and watching the charts not to mention that there was a news story on it just this morning. I have a good feeling about this stock. Besides, I need to bust out in a big way and I have a pretty good feeling that this bad boy is going come through so I can make my whole month back today.

Bill proceeded to place an order to buy 3,000 shares at the market price. Sure enough, his buy order immediately hit the ASK and was filled at 23.46.

Bill: Not a great fill but at least I'm in for the ride. You know, I have been sitting here all day, every day for the past two months and it has done no good. Every time I get a winner, I close the position out too soon because I see a profit and I get over-anxious. I am going to try something new . . . Hey, Mike, I'm hungry—wanna grab some lunch?

Mike *(slightly confused)*: What do you mean lunch? You just on a huge position!

Bill: Yeah I know. That's my new strategy! I'm going to let it breath for a while. So how about lunch?

Mike: Uh, no thanks—I'm going to stick around for a while.

Bill: You sure? Ok, no problem. See you later.

An hour later Bill returned, refreshed from his lunch and happy to see that the stock price had increased from 23.46 to 24.61 (more than $3,000 unrealized profit). Convinced that he had broken the curse that had been placed on his keyboard, he decided that a great new trading style had been discovered.

Bill: Now that's what I'm talking about! You watch, my whole month is coming back on this trade, my whole month! See you tomorrow man!

The next day Mike showed up at his regular time, went through his daily routine, and prepped himself for the opening bell. The bell rang and Bill had still not appeared.

Mike: Man, that merger with Bill's stock must have hit the wires. I bet you he got out during after-hours trading, banked his profit, and is still celebrating. Maybe he is onto something with his new trading style.

After questioning the benefits of his own trading game plan (slow-steady-conservative), Mike began his daily grind. At about 10:30 the market slowed down but there was still no sign of Bill. Just for kicks, Mike then decided to check to see how Bill's huge winner was doing. We think you know what Mike found. The last trade was for 9.53, the high for the day was 14.76, and the low for the day was 8.22. Mike never found out when Bill was able to get out of the trade, or even if he got out of the trade, but two things were certain: the merger never happened and the trading stadium next to Mike was empty for the rest of the year.

All traders at one time or another have made bad trades, but the online trading athletes who make it to the all-star team are the ones who learn from these mistakes. They learn to control their frustration and anger so that they minimize bad trades and increase the frequency of their good trades. Then, if they make a losing trade, they can analyze why it was a loser and use it to modify their game plan and trading strategy, as necessary.

LOSING TRADES

A trade either is profitable or not profitable. There is a natural human tendency to think of all unprofitable trades as bad trades. But it is important to understand that losing trades are not always bad trades. You can execute a series of perfectly good trades, sticking to your game plan, and still lose. This does not mean you are a bad trader, it does mean that you have experienced defeat. A winning online trading athlete focuses on bouncing back from defeat and winning their next game.

Some examples from the sports world might help clarify the important point we are making here. Think about the NFL. When the season ends, there is only one winner left—the Super Bowl champion. That certainly makes them a good team. During the 2000–2001 season, the two Super Bowl finalists thrived on the fact that they did not get much recognition from the national press as having a place among the very best teams. These teams used this as motivation to go out and beat all of the more highly rated teams in the playoffs. It worked! In the final game before the Super Bowl, the New York Giants beat the speedy Minnesota Vikings, 41–0; the Baltimore Ravens beat the favored Oakland Raiders, 16–3.

Does the fact that the Ravens won the Super Bowl in 2001 mean that every other team in the NFL was a bad team? Not at all! In fact, some teams with winning records did not even make the playoffs. But the nature of football, and of all sports, means that even good teams often lose.

The athletes we work with have to learn early in their careers how to handle this. They must learn that when they lose, it does not mean they played badly. They must also learn that when they win, it does not necessarily mean that they played well. They must look beyond winning and losing and learn how to analyze their performance realistically. Without this skill, athletes tend to burn out and quit at an alarming rate, because loss and defeat is such a common part of any competitive environment.

As an online trading athlete, you need to learn how to look at your trades in a similar fashion. Just because you lose on some trades, you must not get down on yourself, or tell yourself that you are a bad trader. An online trading athlete who experiences a series of losing trades will most likely survive in the long run if those losing trades are not also bad trades. However, if you are consistently making bad trades, you will eventually trade yourself out of the game. As an online trading athlete, losing trades are out of your direct control (look back at what we discussed in Chapter 2), while bad trades are something that all trading athletes have control over and can correct.

What about those times when you are making bad trades but they turn out to be winners? If that is your pattern and you are having frequent success doing it, be aware that your trading style does not have a strong foundation. What you have done is reduced the profession of online trading to a coin toss and left your results up to chance. You have become a gambler. Enjoy your gambling hot streak while it lasts, but do not expect to make a career out of sticking to such a game plan. You have based your success on a factor—luck—over which you have no control. It may work out for you for a period of time, but when you leave things solely up to luck, chances are that your funds are going to dwindle and you will find yourself looking for another occupation, often deep in debt.

Mistakes

Mistakes are otherwise known as "Oh - - - -" moments! Sometimes we just make an honest mistake by hitting the wrong button or putting in an order size that is much larger than intended. Everyone has done this at one time or another; it comes with the territory. If you happen to get in a trade via a mistake, do not play around. Get out of the trade immediately.

Kurt, a momentum trader in his mid-30s, has been in the online game for four and a half years. He is no different than most online traders in that it has taken him some time to get his feet wet and he has moments where he questions whether or not he is cut out for this occupation. He had been trading part-time for two years and finally decided that he wanted to give trading a "real try" so he left

his previous job as an engineer and began trading full-time
from his home. At first, Kurt was shocked by how many
hours he was putting in as a trader. When he first decided
to go into trading, he thought for sure that now that he was
his own boss he would be able to cut back on his work hours.
He quickly realized that part-time trading was nothing like
trading full-time. As an engineer, Kurt had a fine eye for detail and a strong analytical background so he focused on his
strengths and began to apply them to the trading game. For
the first six months, he did not make any money, but was re-
silient and despite questioning his career change, continued
to trade full-time. The next six months were not any better
and his confidence began to wear down. What was he doing
wrong? Was he too conservative? Did he need to loosen up
a bit? Maybe trading just was not for him. One Friday afternoon, Kurt closed his last open position of being short 600
shares of WXYZ from 24.18 and packed it up for the week.
He spent the entire weekend evaluating his current situation and wondering if he should maybe begin to look for
other employment. After all, he was realistic in that he did
not expect to get rich quick in trading, but he did not
think that it would take this long for him to get the hang of
it. Also, he had only put aside enough money to support
himself for a year and that time was quickly coming to an
end.

After doing some serious soul searching, Kurt decided to
give trading one more week and if nothing changed, then
he would close shop and write this trading thing off as a
learning experience. Kurt began his Monday morning as he
always did by preparing for the trading day. To his shock, as
he reviewed his trading statement from last week, he realized that he had not only closed out his short position in
WXYZ, but had mistakenly overbought and was still long
5,400 shares from 24.73. Realizing that he must have bought
6,000 shares rather than 600 shares to flatten himself out,

he began to panic. Even fully margined, there was barely enough equity in his account to cover that trade. Was he going to get a margin call? Was the statement right? How could he have made such a careless error? Panicked, he turned his computer on to find out what WXYZ's opening call was. As he waited for his computer to load up he began to imagine the worst-case scenario: "What if WXYZ is down a couple of points? I can't believe this is happening to me! No one is going to care that I made an honest mistake, I'll still need to make good on the trade."

To Kurt's astonishment, WXYZ's opening call was 27.95 bid–28.24 offer. A nervous sigh of relief came over him. He could not believe that his simple mistake, which could have cost him tens of thousands of dollars ended up being a more than $16,000 winner. Boy, did he get lucky.

This traumatic experience woke Kurt up and helped him realize how close he had come to financial disaster. After careful consideration, he decided to stick with trading for another couple of months (even though he knew his new-found success was dumb luck) to see if he could turn things around. During that time, he began to find his niche and went on to continue his career as an online trading athlete. Today, one year later, Kurt is a seasoned online trading athlete who enjoys a significant amount of success in the trading game. Although his mistake ended up "jumpstarting" his trading career, whenever he tells his story, he makes sure to stress that although mistakes are just another part of the game and can sometimes be an added plus, most often mistakes are an expensive negative.

As this story illustrates, it is sometimes possible to get lucky and have a mistake trade turn into a winner. However, successful online trading athletes, such as Kurt, recognize mistakes for what they are: a violation of their game plan and a threat to their strategy. Kurt got lucky and he realized it. Once again, let us repeat: an online trading athlete is not a gambler. If you are lucky enough to make some money off a mistake, remind yourself of how lucky you have been. As an online trading athlete, you can think of these rare occurrences as payback for when you made a good trade but it turned out to be a loser. This is similar to how a batter views hits that come from those "bleeders" or "balls with eyes." He sees these lucky hits as payback for the line drives he has hit back to the pitcher for an out.

Now let us talk about how to maintain a winning attitude in the face of losing trades, and how to keep the right focus that will prevent you from making bad trades.

POSITIVE TRADING ATTITUDE

Sport psychologists have found that successful athletes have a positive mental attitude (PMA) toward competition, while we have found that online trading athletes who continually achieve success have what we call a positive trading attitude (PTA). This attitude is what helps successful traders overcome even a series of losing trades and prevent bad trades.

What is a PTA? To help explain PTA, let us look once again at the game of baseball. Because of the nature of the game, baseball hitters frequently experience disappointing performances. Even when they are hitting the ball well, good defense can make their lives miserable. Occasionally, hitting slumps last for extended periods of time and turn into performance slumps. An example of this would be a hitter who during the month of July is tearing the cover off the ball and ends up hitting .345. Then, unexpectedly, during the next month, he is not getting the same pop off the bat and the fielders seem to always be in the way. As a result, he finishes the month of August hitting .125. A baseball player with a PMA views his drop in batting average from .345 last month to .125 this month as a temporary drop in performance rather than as proof that he is a bad player. PMA is not just a cool acronym: it is essential for achieving performance excellence.

Similarly, a trading athlete who cleaned up last month, but has had two losing weeks in a row will be able to survive this tough time better if he or she has a PTA. A trading athlete with a PTA sees the past few weeks as a learning experience, an obstacle to overcome, rather than as a signal that he or she is in the wrong business.

Having a PTA means that you truly believe in your game plan. It is more than just keeping your chin up during tough times. It is about believing in yourself and your game plan in the face of adversity. Trading, just like athletic competition, means that you have to learn how to handle failure. Failure is a major aspect of sports and trading. In competition, one team or person wins while the other loses. In trading, a trade is either a winner or a loser. The difference between success and failure for both athletes and traders is more about one's ability to deal with and overcome failure than it is about native talent.

Online trading athletes actually have it a little easier than competitive athletes when facing adversity. Competitive athletes have to deal with adversaries who are committed, heart and soul, to defeating them. In sports, your opponent will make every effort to prevent you from succeeding. Online trading athletes only have to deal with the market, which is impersonal. The market does not care if your trades are winners and losers, it only seems that way to you sometimes.

Now perhaps you are sitting back and saying to yourself, "Yeah this is nice, I've heard it before, but how do I really learn how to use PTA?" This is an excellent question. A lot of people think they know what PTA is, but few really know how to implement it on a daily basis. For example, having a PTA does not mean that you blindly try to think positively at all times. Let us explain what we mean.

WHY POSITIVE THINKING IS NOT ENOUGH

Both of us have heard many motivational speeches during our years of consulting. A common theme of many motivational speeches is that if you can just imagine yourself succeeding, you will succeed. "Imagine fulfilling your greatest dream and if you really believe you can do it, the dream will come true," shouted one motivational expert.

What nonsense! Do you mean to tell us that the next time some golfer is buried in the sand trap, if he just begins to think positive that he will be able to blast out of the sand in Tiger Woods-like fashion and land two feet from the cup saving par? We do not think so!

The truth is that positive thinking by itself will not make anyone a better athlete or better trader. Hard work is what allows a person to reach his or her goals, and there is no substitute for effort and practice in both trading and sports. No one gets rich at trading by taking it easy or by playing the market casually. You either take time to learn the market and develop your trading style or you do not survive. The equation is cruel but simple.

The problem with positive thinking is clearly summarized by shooter Bob Foth. Bob is one of our country's greatest shooters, and has won several World Cup events and a silver medal at the 1992 Olympics in Barcelona.

"How can it be true that I am supposed to 'think positively' all the time?" he asked. "I spend hours practicing every day, and I often have to be very critical of myself. I have to catch my own mistakes, notice if my form is wrong, I have to be very hard on myself to keep improving my technique and focus. If I have any weaknesses, I have to spot them and get rid of them. When I'm up there on the line, I need to know that I'm a stronger shooter, that I'm a better prepared athlete than the next guy. I can't afford weaknesses. What good would it do me to always think positively? What I need to learn is how to be more objectively critical of myself."

This honest athlete pinpointed the problem with the myth of positive thinking. If we want to keep improving in life we need to identify our weaknesses and deficiencies. Only then can we figure out how to improve. Instead of just positive thinking, this requires the type of thinking we have identified as being often found in successful people—the ability to be critical without also being negative. This is the secret of a PTA.

Good traders stick to their game plans and play to their strengths. Great traders do this also, but in addition, they identify their weaknesses and work diligently to overcome them. Some of the most successful traders we know have actually made their weaknesses into strengths. They do this by listening to that little voice in their heads that tells them when they are making a mistake, and then using that information to avoid making that mistake again. This internal voice is something we all have. Sport psychologists call it self-talk, and it is one of the most powerful strategies used by successful athletes.

SELF-TALK

Have you ever noticed that you spend a lot of time talking to yourself? This is not a sign of impending madness; it is simply the way our verbal minds operate. Often our thinking takes place through a sort of internal self-dialogue. It is as if you are listening to two people having a conversation:

"Hmmm, I can't believe how low QCOM has fallen. Maybe now is a good time to buy?"

"Are you kidding yourself? Remember how you got burned the last time you went into QCOM?"

"Yes, but the numbers look solid now. I think it's definitely trending up."

"I don't know, I hate to lose money on a stock like that."

And so on.

Often the inner voice in your head is negative and demanding. We call this internal voice "The Critic." This voice is almost automatic, popping into your head without warning to make you miserable. It is how you handle your internal Critic that defines your success in the skill of self-talk.

Much of the skill of self-talk comes from being able to identify the typical negative thoughts of your Critic, then replacing them with productive thoughts that will help you perform your best. We all have typical patterns of negative thinking, born out of our experiences in childhood and adolescence.

Here is a good way you can start to identify the thoughts that interfere with your performance. This method was used by sport psychology researchers Sue Jackson and Glyn Roberts of the University of Illinois to help collegiate athletes discover the impact of their inner voice. They asked 200 college athletes what they were thinking about during their very best and their very worst performances.

Jackson and Roberts found that during their best performance ever, 66 percent of the athletes were thinking about the performance itself. They were concentrating on what they were doing. For example, one tennis player described her thoughts during her best match: "I wrote down some goals before the match. One was to really enjoy myself and the other was to be completely focused on the ball. I was going to try to achieve these goals and not worry about the outcome. I was trying to play one point at a time and focus on the ball, to really try to see the ball. I was confident but not really thinking about winning or losing—I was totally engrossed in the task at hand. Nothing else existed. Just me, the ball, and nothing else. So, I played in total control."

When they described their worst performances ever, an amazing 88 percent of the athletes said they were worrying about the result of their competition. They were so focused on the outcome of their event, they were not able to concentrate on what they were doing. For example, one runner described his thoughts during the race like this: "In the back of my mind, I was thinking, 'I'm not that good, do I really belong up here?' Running the race I was not focused at all. I was looking everywhere. I remember at one point thinking that I should be up further. I thought, 'Well, what does it matter, you're not going to qualify anyway.' Instead of concentrating on the task at hand, I let the fear of outcome paralyze me."

You can use the same method to begin to identify the self-defeating thoughts that interfere with your own chances of success. Try the following exercise yourself.

IDENTIFY YOUR NEGATIVE THOUGHTS

Think about your typical trading day. How do you approach your workday? How do you handle your trades? Now think back to a recent time when you were trading at a high level. Your performance was excellent. We want you to write down a list of the things you were saying to yourself in that situation.

To get you started, here is a list of some of the thoughts that our clients have had during their best performances and were willing to share with us over the years.

- Get involved. Jump in and start small.
- I feel focused and ready for anything.
- I found my rhythm. Keep it up!
- Stay patient and relaxed.
- I am all over this market. Where is my next profit? Bring it on.
- Everything I touch turns into a winner. I am unstoppable!
- I am on autopilot. Seeing the opportunity and reacting.
- I am just surfing the wave and pulling in the cash!

Now, think of a recent bad experience. Remember a recent situation in which your performance was poor and you were disappointed at the way you handled the situation. Now, write down what you were saying to yourself in that situation. Once again we have listed the thoughts that some of our clients have shared with us over the years about their performances:

- Yesterday was lousy. I really need a big day today.
- Everyone else is making a lot of money this week. What is wrong with me?
- This trade is making me nervous. I am backing out now before I get really burned.
- I am not sure if I should make this trade.
- I feel like I am getting chewed up by the bid and ask.
- The market is reading my mind.
- My rhythm is totally off. Everything is moving too fast.
- I hope this trade turns around or I am in real trouble.
- I have got too much exposure. I do not know whether I am long or short.

By tuning into your self-talk, your inner voice, you will be able to identify patterns of thought that are effective for you and types of thought that hurt your performance. This knowledge will enable you to develop a PTA. For example, a number of our clients learned that when they were alert, focused, and stayed involved in a limited number of positions, they performed well. When they thought about how much money they were losing or how they felt inside, they traded poorly. The point is, once you can identify your negative self-talk, you can begin to do something about it.

PUT YOUR CRITIC TO WORK

It might surprise you to learn that you can use your Critic in very helpful ways. How? By using your Critic to identify weaknesses so that you can figure out ways to improve. The Critic is persuasive because it is partially right. "Don't mess up this trade like you did last time," it shouts. It is true that the last time you shorted this stock you got burned. But you are a different person now. You have learned new skills, which make you a better trader. Only your Critic does not know you have changed.

So use your Critic to help you improve. Look realistically at your negative thoughts. Write them down. Is there a problem here? Could you improve this area? Then go ahead and do so. Often the way to combat poor trading performances is to learn the skills you need to be a better, more complete trader. Once the problem is identified (thanks to the Critic), you are in a position to do something about it. Perhaps you can attend a workshop to improve your analysis skills. Perhaps a colleague who is a talented momentum trader will agree to work with you to help your approach. Maybe you are always second-guessing yourself, if so, you need to find a trading coach to help you get back in the game. There are many possible solutions. But you will only reach those solutions if you deal with the negative thoughts of the Critic.

Recognize that the Critic is based in your past, not your present. Once you have improved, your Critic will take a while to catch up with the new you. When you make mistakes, acknowledge them and recognize that you have identified an area where you have problems. Resolve to learn what you need to so that the problem does not happen again. Then stop worrying about it! If you realistically decide that you do not need to improve in an area, learn to ignore your Critic.

How can you ignore your Critic while you are performing? Well, that is the next step in mastering successful self-talk. Once you have learned to use your Critic to help you, it is still important to reduce your negative thinking, especially in performance situations.

REPLACE NEGATIVITY WITH PRODUCTIVITY

To trade at your best, day in and day out, you must replace negative thinking (which interferes with good performance) with productive thinking (which promotes excellence). Successful people find that when they reduce their negative thoughts, they are more likely to achieve their goals. Now, we are going to show you how to do the same thing.

The best way to eliminate unwanted negative thoughts is to focus on desired productive thoughts. Train your mind to notice negative thoughts and to replace them immediately with productive ones. Let us see how it is done.

Go back to the list of negative thoughts you collected in the best and worst thoughts exercise. Take a blank page. Draw a line down the middle. On the left-hand side, write down your negative thoughts in that situation. On the right-hand side, write down a helpful thought for each of those hurtful thoughts. Think about the best way to counteract each negative thought.

Here are some examples for a trader who has moved into full-time trading after two years of successful part-time trading.

Negative Thought	Productive Thought
This will be a disaster.	This is a great chance to do something I enjoy and am good at.
I am not good enough to trade full-time.	I have been successful so far. I need to stick to my plan.
My stomach is in knots. I feel awful.	I am excited to be doing this. It is normal to have butterflies.
I am not sure if I should make that trade.	I have worked hard and proven myself. I can do this and be successful.
What if this trade turns out to be a loser?	Winning and losing is a natural and necessary part of this game and I get better as I go.

Take some time to come up with a list of productive thoughts that will really work for you. Experiment. If you come up with some self-talk that is better than what you have been using, try it. Ask others for advice. Carry a notebook around with you and keep jotting down ideas for improving your self-talk and developing a strong PTA.

The next step is to become comfortable with your PTA. Repetition is the best approach. Never utter a negative thought without replacing it with a productive one.

Whenever you catch yourself thinking negatively (and you will), start thinking productively instead. Do not get upset if you are still thinking negatively even after practice. Remember, it took years for you to get where you are today. Calmly stop the negative thought and start a productive thought. You will be amazed at how much your trading can improve when you master a solid PTA.

This technique is simple to learn but takes time to master. The keys are to select the words you use during your self-talk strategy carefully and to know when to use them. Some common self-talk phrases that we have all been guilty of using at one time or another might include, "C'mon, you know better than that," or "I can't believe I did that," or "Man, was that stupid, I really stink."

The key to self-talk is word selection. Positive and effective self-talk uses words like "can," "do," "will," "control," and "prepared" and avoids words like "hope," "cannot," and "unable." Whichever positive words you choose, they should have meaning to you and remind you of your greatest performances.

An example of positive self-talk in baseball is when the bases are loaded, the score is tied, there are two outs, and as he steps to the plate the batter says to himself, "I am in control. I have trained for this. I am going to see the ball and hit the ball."

An example of positive self-talk in golf is when a golfer is eight feet from the cup, putting for birdie to win the hole, and he says to himself, "Focus. I have made this shot hundreds of times. Swing straight through the ball and hear it land in the cup."

In both of these examples, the athletes are mentally preparing themselves for their performance. They have chosen to use positive words like "control" and "focus" coupled with specific phrases such as "see the ball, hit the ball" or "swing straight through" that have a deeper meaning for them. Both athletes also recognize the appropriate moment in time to use their self-talk strategy because they are entering a pressure situation where they want to tap into their peak performance so they can achieve success.

An example of positive self-talk for trading athletes is when they are in the market, looking for opportunities and say to themselves, "Stay patient and in control. When the indicators appear, I am going to react and attack. Wait for it, there it is, go for it."

In contrast, an example of destructive self-talk is after an online trading athlete makes a bad trade and says to himself or herself, "I am such an idiot. I can't believe I did that. I really stink."

Self-talk, if positive and effective, can be a powerful weapon for the trading athlete; however, if negative and destructive, it can prove to be an athlete's most dangerous enemy.

By adding positive self-talk to your game plan, you will be able to experience the PTA that successful athletes have. Remember, when you keep a positive frame of mind, adversity begins to melt way. If applied correctly, self-talk can be an extremely effective tool to help you focus and perform consistently in the face of adversity. In the next chapter, we show you how to apply these self-talk skills and your PTA to overcome the stress that seems to be a regular part of the high-pressure world of the online trading athlete.

How Winners Handle Losing

- Use self-talk
- Maintain a positive trading attitude (PTA)
- Why positive thinking is not enough
- Identify your negative thoughts
- Put your Critic to work
- Replace negativity with productivity

CHAPTER FIVE

HOW TO ENERGIZE, NOT CATASTROPHIZE, IN PRESSURE SITUATIONS

Lyz is an experienced online trader. She is used to the highs and lows of following the market. Still, there are certain moments that are very stressful. Such a moment comes when she has done a lot of research on a stock and sees a great opportunity one day when it bounces off a support level. She bides her time, waiting for the right moment, and then makes her move—a much bigger move than usual because she feels so strongly that this is a great opportunity. But her stomach goes into free fall when the stock suddenly dips sharply soon after her trade. She hangs on and waits for the uptick, but it does not happen. She feels her muscles tightening and the sweat gathering on her forehead and under her arms. How much longer should she hang on? Should she just write it off or should she take a longer position? When is the right time to make a move? She can feel the stress increasing by the moment.

Pressure is an everyday part of the online trading athlete's world. It is a normal part of any competitive environment, and this includes the world of trading as much as any football field or hockey rink. What separates the average player from the all-star is how he or she deals with this pressure. When we allow the situation we are in to dictate our responses, we experience high stress, which has a detrimental effect and leads to poor performance and eventually to burnout. But believe it or not, pressure can also give you the edge that you need to stay ahead of the game. Instead of becoming stressed-out, successful athletes learn to energize themselves in high-pressure situations. This is a skill that you must also develop. Your ability to handle high-pressure situations will be the deciding factor in how successful you are as an online trading athlete.

PRESSURE: HOW DO YOU LOOK AT IT?

Two great American sprinters, Carl and Reid, are preparing for the same race, the Olympic Trials. The top three finishers will go on to the Olympics. Everyone else goes home and waits another four years for their chance. Carl seems nervous and jumpy as he waits for the call to the blocks. He keeps looking around distractedly, and when the race starts he is too tense. He finishes sixth. Reid is cool and composed as he awaits the starter's signal. When the race begins he has tunnel vision, ignoring all distractions, and he wins the race and qualifies for the Olympics. How can we analyze the difference between these two great sprinters?

Both are under the same pressure, that of qualifying for the Olympics. The race is surely the same for both of them. Yet one is tense and anxious and performs poorly, while the other is focused and confident and performs well. Are they both experiencing the same stress? Clearly the important race itself is not the only source of stress.

In Chapter 4, we discussed how self-talk makes all the difference in determining whether you have a positive trading attitude (PTA) or not. This same self-talk will decide whether you experience stress in a pressure situation. Self-talk was the critical difference between Carl and Reid. Before the race, Carl was saying to himself, "I can't believe this is the Olympic Trials. I've been training eight years for this. I must win this race. If I don't go to the Olympics I will let everyone down. I'll never get another chance. Don't blow it."

Reid, however, was talking to himself in a different manner. He was saying, "This is your big chance. You have trained for this moment, go out and take it. I'm feeling uptight, which is a good thing, because this means a lot to me. Focus on getting off to a good start and then hitting my rhythm quickly. Explode out of the blocks."

Is it any wonder that Carl feels stressed and tense before the race? His own words to himself focus on the negative aspects of the race ("I *must* win this race," "I'll let everybody down"). He emphasizes the pressure. Reid instead focuses on factors under his control (his start, his rhythm) and acknowledges the pressure while normalizing it ("I'm feeling uptight, which is a good thing, because this means a lot to me"). The words we use to talk to ourselves in pressure situations are critical in shaping our emotional reactions to these events. How we react emotionally will, in turn, shape our performance in critical situations.

HOW TO DEAL WITH PRESSURE

For an NBA player to be ready to play a 48-minute game, racing up and down the hardwood floor, they must stay in superb physical shape. They train hard to be ready for the

strenuous demands of the pro game. Online trading athletes must also be prepared for the rigors of their chosen
profession. They must train hard to deal with the ups and
downs of the market, and they have to be prepared to handle the pressures of trading.

Of course, what causes one person stress may not be
hard to handle for another. For example, one trader may
become nervous in anticipation of quarterly earnings on a
stock in his sector while in the same situation another trader
may feed off the energy of that moment and feel more
confident. To clarify this situation further, the following is
a useful exercise that gives you a chance to list the situations
and behaviors that cause you the most stress.

IDENTIFYING THE SOURCES OF STRESS IN YOUR TRADING LIFE

We asked a friend of ours, Jared, who is a successful trader,
to make a list of the aspects of his trading day that he finds
most stressful. Here is the list he came up with.

WHAT JARED FINDS MOST STRESSFUL ABOUT TRADING

- Getting caught in a fast market
- Unexpected news releases
- Sudden major market fluctuations for no apparent reason
- Hearing about another trader who has blown his account out
- Not spending enough time with my family
- Slow executions of my orders

Now, think about the things that really weigh on you during your trading day. In what situations do you feel the most pressure? What causes you the most stress? Write your answers down below.

WHAT YOU FIND MOST STRESSFUL ABOUT TRADING

_____

_____

_____

_____

_____

_____

You will make use of this list throughout this chapter. In the pages that follow, as we show you how to handle pressure and reduce stress, apply the strategies you learn to the above situations. Keep asking yourself how you can do better in handling your most stressful situations. Also, you may add to this list as time goes on. You may encounter new sources of stress, or rediscover a stressful situation that you had forgotten about. When you do, add it to the list above and date your addition so you can track changes over time.

Whether these pressures lead to a stressed-out trading athlete or an energized trading athlete depends on the self-talk of the trader. Online trading athletes do not need to be in the same superb physical shape as an NBA player (although staying fit helps), but they must have their minds prepared to deal with the inevitable pressures of the trading lifestyle. How can you prepare mentally to reduce the stress you experience as an online trading athlete, and to achieve your highest levels of performance? We suggest a three-step approach to handling the pressures and anxieties of life as a trader.

1. Use energizing self-talk instead of stressful self-talk.
2. Take time-outs when you need them.
3. Build regular recovery time into your trading life.

Now let us look at each step in turn.

ENERGIZING SELF-TALK

POSITIVE SELF-TALK = ENERGY

Positive self-talk facilitates energized feeling and performance whereas negative self-talk causes stress and results in lower physical energy and quicker fatigue. Self-talk, therefore, needs to be directed because depending on whether it is positive or negative, it can make you feel either powerful and prepared, or tired and lethargic.

"I am feeling good this morning. I had a great night's sleep and I am ready to dive into the market. It is going to be a great day today. The market better show some volatility because I am coming to play ball!"

NEGATIVE SELF-TALK = LETHARGY

"(Yawn) I should not have gone to bed so late. I feel beat. I cannot wait until this day is over so I can get some rest. Boy, are my shoulders tight. I really should get a massage after the market closes. I hope it's a quiet day today because I do not feel like doing much."

As both of these short dialogues show, creating high mental energy can help you achieve good results while creating negative mental energy most often leads to poor or lackluster performance.

Pressure situations require lots of energy. Just as the NBA player needs high physical and mental energy to go hard for 48 minutes every night, the online trading athlete requires high positive mental energy to maintain focus, overcome self-defeating thoughts, and deal with the many distractions of the trader's life. Unfortunately, when stress begins to build up, athletes often focus on how nervous, tense, or tired they feel. The stress reaction is often exaggerated by dwelling on it, thereby creating even more stress and negative energy. Carl experienced this before the start of his race, and ran poorly as a result. In exactly the same way, online trading athletes increase their feelings of stress by focusing on thoughts of inadequacy and by ruminating about the possible consequences of performing poorly.

Fortunately, positive and negative self-talk have a reciprocal relationship. Whenever the frequency of positive self-talk is high the incidence of negative self-talk is low. The goal of a PTA is to lower negative self-talk and increase positive self-talk. Reid did this before the start of his race. Although he was aware of the stress response in reaction to the pressure of the Olympic Trials, he told himself that this was normal and reminded himself to focus on factors he could control. To maintain a PTA for yourself, you must learn to substitute realistic and constructive self-talk for the bad habits that create negative energy and feelings.

One technique to alter the thinking patterns that create high stress is energizing. Once you realize that you are having negative thoughts, yell "Stop!" to yourself, and then replace the energy-diminishing thoughts with energy-enhancing ones. Energizing works by disrupting the flow of negative thoughts, enabling you to shift attention to more rational and productive thoughts. This technique will not work unless you have developed energizing thoughts to replace the negative ones. As you learned in Chapter 4, it is beneficial to list your most common negative thoughts and how you would counter them with thoughts that help keep you focused and energized. Below are some suggestions that should help you use your self-talk as an energizing force.

USE POSITIVE SELF-TALK THAT IS BASED IN REALITY

Two good sources of realistic positive self-statements are your previous performances and your preparation. For example, "I have dealt with unexpected losses like this before and I have come through in the crunch, I know I can do it again today"; or "I have prepared very well for these types of trading situations, I am physically and mentally strong, I am prepared, now all I have to do is let myself perform to my potential." You know better than anyone how to energize yourself in pressure situations. You therefore need to practice, and practice convincingly. Dwelling on mistakes, setbacks, or feelings of anxiety makes it more difficult for you to energize yourself. Instead focus on the positive things you have done and remind yourself that you have worked hard to get where you are today and that you have overcome the stress before and can again today.

Focus on Your Goals

To help cope with the stress reaction to pressure, focus on your goals, on what you want to accomplish, and how you are going to accomplish it. For example say to yourself "Remember my goals, I have the ability and determination to achieve them. Nothing can stop me." Go back over the goals you created for yourself in Chapter 2. Display them prominently in your trading stadium so you can refer to them when you begin to feel distracted or overwhelmed.

Sometimes the hardest part of dealing with stress is breaking the cycle of feeling anxious, which creates thoughts of failure, which worsens the feelings of nervousness. That is why we suggest using a personal time-out system to interrupt the stress reaction and return to a focused and energized state.

Time-Outs

Most competitive sports use time-outs. This provides the athlete with an opportunity to regroup and refocus. In basketball, a time-out is called by the coach and lasts for perhaps a minute. For the golfer, a time-out can be the few seconds that he or she takes to wipe off the face of the club. For a baseball or softball player it could be stepping out of the box and putting pine tar on the bat or talc on their hands. These precious few seconds in competition can be maximized if the athlete spends them focusing on his or her next shot or next pitch, rather than worrying about stressful outside distractions. To show you what we are talking about, let us take a closer look at an example of using time-outs in baseball.

Baseball players who stay at the top of their game realize the importance of calling a personal time-out when stress builds up and they need to refocus. To the average observer or even the average player, a hitter's at-bat does not start until the ball is thrown. This is far from the truth. The elite baseball player knows that there is a power struggle going on even before a pitch is thrown, and that whoever is more in control before the ball is thrown, is more likely to end up winning the conflict. The following example illustrates our point.

Bob (the pitcher) is on the mound as Mike (the batter) steps up to the plate, and the power struggle begins. Mike finds a comfortable stance and begins to focus on the release point of the ball while maintaining a little internal rhythm, moving back and forth, to keep his momentum and stay loose. He is ready to react and explode in a split second. Waiting, waiting, waiting—the pressure builds, he begins to tighten up, and he starts thinking about the score. His team needs a rally in this inning. He has become distracted. The ball is released and Mike is a fraction of a second late. The result is that the pitcher wins this battle because Mike is unable to produce (i.e., he grounds or pops out). What happened to Mike? He lost control of the at-bat because the pitcher forced him to wait. So the real question is:

What could he have done to remain loose and in control?

An option available to Mike and to most athletes is to call a personal time-out. Imagine the same situation again. Mike feels the stress piling up while he is waiting, waiting, waiting—but this time he lifts his hand up and says, "Time-out blue." The umpire responds by calling time-out. Mike then steps out of the batter's box, gaining control of the situation and allowing himself to release the stress and refocus. He takes a deep breath, reminds himself to have "quick hands," and then reenters the batter's box having regained his internal rhythm, relaxed and prepared to explode. Bob begins his motion and releases the ball, but this time Mike reacts instantly and makes solid contact. The result is that Mike wins this interaction by producing a quality at-bat simply because he minimized his stress level and took control of the at-bat before the ball was thrown.

How does this performance strategy translate to the situation of the online trading athlete? First, think of yourself as the hitter and the market as the pitcher. Just like the hitter, your level of stress before the ball (sector you are following) is thrown has a tremendous effect on whether you will make solid contact (make a quality trade) or not. Most traders have experienced the unwelcome sensation of falling into what we call a trading trance. You lose focus and just sit there, staring at the bids and offers and the colors flashing on the screen. It is impossible to make great decisions if you have fallen into a trading trance. Similarly, Lyz, the trader we began this chapter discussing, found it hard to think clearly when she allowed herself to become totally stressed by a big trade. In these situations, it is imperative that the online trading athlete blows the whistle and calls a time-out. Just like our hitter, Mike, you must step away for a second to minimize the stress and refocus. As an online trading athlete, you have the opportunity to call a time-out for yourself whenever you need it, so take advantage of this to adjust your game plan and refocus your thoughts whenever necessary.

Time-outs are great ways to break up negative patterns and help you find your trading rhythm. Play the game rather than letting the game play you. The hardest part about calling a time-out is realizing when you need it and being disciplined enough to use it. We understand that as a competitor, you do not want to take yourself out of the action, not even for a second, because you think you might miss that great opportunity that is going to turn things around for you or take you to the next level. This is a perfectly normal and natural way to feel, but in the end, if you want to become an all-star, you are going to have to stop looking for that one grand slam homerun and instead trust your skills to achieve excellence gradually. Do not worry: the money will still be there tomorrow. The only real question is are you going to be making it or losing it?

Let us now take a look at some concrete examples of the use of time-outs combined with energizing self-talk to transform potentially negative situations into winning scenarios. First, we will look at some of the ways athletes from different sports might use personal time-outs to deal with pressure situations.

Golfer

Stressed

"Man it's hot out here. What hole are we on? The sixth! That's all? I'm beat!"

Take a Personal Time-Out!

Energized

"It's hot out here. Time to drink some water to stay hydrated. Refocus. Now I'm ready to grip-n-rip."

Softball Player

Stressed

"This pitcher is tough! I can't keep up. My swing is slow and my bat feels like it weighs a ton!"

Take a Personal Time-Out!

Energized

"My bat feels light and quick. I am ready to drill the next pitch."

Tennis Player

Stressed

"My serve is just not working today. I'm a lousy net player."

Take a Personal Time-Out!

Energized

"I belong out here. Stay alert and keep exploiting my opponent's weaknesses."

Basketball Player

Stressed

"That guy keeps going around me! I feel like my feet are stuck to the ground."

Take a Personal Time-Out!

Energized

"I'm sticking to him like glue. My legs feel springy and the floor feels like a trampoline."

Just as they are for competitive athletes, time-outs and energizing thoughts are an important weapon for success for the online trading athlete. They can mean the difference between just going through the motions and making bad trades or reacting properly to the moment and going for the kill.

We hope you enjoyed these examples from the world of sports. Now let us use our formula for taking a time-out and energizing for the trading game.

Online Trading Athlete

Stressed

"Everything I touch turns to garbage. I have lousy luck."

Take a Personal Time-Out!

Energized

"I am the same winner I was last week. I will be patient and work gradually to get my rhythm back."

Stressed

"I can't believe I made that trade. What was I thinking? I knew it was going to be a loser."

Take a Personal Time-Out!

Energized

"I have to stick to my trading plan. I just made a mistake. What did I learn? Avoid playing my hunches. Stick to the game plan."

Are you getting the hang of it? Good! Because now, its time for you to step into the batting cage and practice creating some energizing thoughts for typical stressful situations.

Stressed

"I'm not concentrating today. What's wrong with me? I have to try harder."

Take a Personal Time-Out!

Energized

"_____"

Stressed

"Every trade I make immediately goes against me."

Take a Personal Time-Out!

Energized

"_____"

Stressed

"How many more losers can I take? I just don't care anymore. I hate the market."

Take a Personal Time-Out!

Energized

"_____"

Now that you know how to use time-outs and energizing thoughts to deal with pressure and reduce stress, we turn to the final piece of the puzzle—keeping your body in good shape to deal with the rigors of the trading lifestyle. Energizing thinking is a great skill to learn but it is not a magic potion. Without taking care of your body, you are not going to be successful over the long term. Therefore, as an online trading athlete, you also need to make sure that you stay physically well rested and properly nourished. This means getting an adequate amount of sleep every night and eating several nutritious meals throughout the trading day. Very competitive people often become so wrapped up in their work that they end up skipping breakfast and/or lunch and staying up late and rising early. We are not going to sugar-coat this—such a pattern of behavior is sure to lead to poor performances. There may be some temporary short-term gains to be had by burning the candle at both ends, but over the long term, poor eating habits and poor sleep patterns cause people to become irritable and distracted, thereby preventing them from performing at the top of their game. The final aspect of reducing stress and performing at your peak is to learn the fundamentals of rest and recovery.

REST AND RECOVERY

You are going into battle 8 to 10 hours a day, 5 days a week. (Some of you die-hard trading athletes are in the game even longer!) For this reason, it is critical that you manage your recovery time, and the truth is, it is something that we all know but rarely do.

Elite athletes who make it to the Hall of Fame have learned how to maximize their recovery time by playing long and hard and recovering quickly and efficiently. As an online trading athlete, think of it this way: when you are in the game waiting for the pitcher to throw the ball, focus on the pitch. When the game is done for the day, relax and take full advantage of this precious but brief recovery time. That means when today's game is over, *do something else* until it is time to put your uniform back on tomorrow. Watch a movie, spend time with loved ones, read a book, work out, go out to eat, and so on. Your long-term success depends on how well you are able to recover between games so that your batteries are recharged when the market opens again.

If it helps, think of each trading day as a round of golf. When you finish a round of golf, what do you do? You go grab a drink, maybe some food, and then you go home, shower, and rest. As an online trading athlete, try to trade with the same discipline that you have when you finish playing golf for the day. Whether or not you had a great round or a terrible one, you realize that it was just today's score and that tomorrow is a whole new game, for better or worse. Keep that same perspective as an online trading athlete.

To help you further understand this, we want to tell you a brief story about a client of ours named Matt, who has been trading online for more than two years. Matt was a former Division I college baseball player who eventually found his way to the career of online trading. Like most other new traders, he had a difficult time transitioning into the trading game. He went through the usual rites of passage: loss of confidence, frustration, anxiety, and high levels of stress. Today he classifies himself as an intermediate trader and has the profit and loss to back it up (clearing $15,000 to $20,000 per month).

Just one short year ago, Matt spent the first 10 months of his rookie season not making a penny; in fact, he lost about $3,000 per month. He questioned whether he had made the right decision leaving a secure job selling mutual funds. Every day he would go to work wondering if he had what it took to be successful at the trading game. If he had a tough day in the market, he would go home when the market closed and immediately go to his apartment, unplug his phone, and crawl onto the couch—depressed, angry, and counting the minutes until the market opened the next day so he could make his money back. He said that the worst part of the experience was that, "If I ended up losing money on a Friday, then my whole weekend went to hell. I would spend the whole weekend pissed off and thinking about Monday morning. I was miserable to be around."

Matt admits that the main difference between how he trades today compared to how he traded a year ago, when he was questioning his ability, is that he has learned how to manage his stress and maximize his down time.

Before, if he had a bad day, he would just take the train home and not want to talk to anyone. Now, regardless of what kind of day he has, he always goes for a jog immediately after the market closes. If he trades nonstop from opening to close, you can be sure that he will be taking a long jog after work to burn off the tension. If, however, it is a slow day then he might cut down his running to about 20 to 30 minutes. It is all about balance.

"You know, it's funny now that I think about it—it works both ways, if I have a bad day, I am able to get it out of my system so that I am not weighed down by it for the rest of the night or weekend. If I have a good day in the market, then I am able to work off the stress that builds up throughout my normal trading day. Either way, I have found that I have more energy and am more prepared and focused to enter the game the next day."

As Matt's story illustrates, the harder and longer you go, the more time you are going to need to recover. Our bodies are designed to recharge every night so your body works kind of like the IRS, "You can pay me now or you can pay me later, but either way, you are going to pay me."

Perhaps you are the competitive type and think that rest and recovery are a waste of time? Well, please think again. It is only your ego that is telling you that if you step out of the game, for even a minute, then you are going to miss that great opportunity that is going to turn your day, week, or even year around.

After all, the market was being played, and money was being won and lost long before you were even born, and it is not going away any time soon. If you are always searching for that lucky break in the form of a 500-foot homerun, a hole in one, or a million-dollar trade, then it may be time for you to start sending some resumes out.

Sure, take your swings at the plate but be patient and wait for your pitch. When the last out is made and today's game is over, focus on energizing yourself for tomorrow's game rather than daydreaming about missed opportunities and what could have been. Of course, learn from your mistakes, but remember, they are just mistakes so move on. Avoid dwelling on them because there are still a lot of games left in the season.

Here is the bottom line: pressure is an integral part of competition, and what separates the mediocre from the elite athlete is their ability to deal with that pressure and not become highly stressed. The same is true for you. Understanding how and when to use time-outs, energizing, and rest and recovery will help you reach your peak potential as an online trading athlete.

How to Energize, Not Catastrophize, in Pressure Situations

- Pressure: How do you look at it?

- How to deal with pressure

- Identifying the sources of stress in your trading life

- Energizing self-talk

  - — Use energizing self-talk instead of stressful talk
  - — Use positive self-talk that is based in reality
  - — Focus on your goals
  - — Take time-outs when you need them
  - — Build regular recovery time into your trading life

- Rest and recovery

CHAPTER SIX

TRADING FOR REVENGE: A RECIPE FOR DISASTER

When discussing trading for revenge with online traders, we sometimes hear the argument that it is impossible to change your personality as a trader. As one trader in Los Angeles said to us, "A leopard can't change its spots." That is, if you have a history of getting upset and angry over losing trades, then you will always act that way when the market goes against you.

The most important question to ask yourself if you want to stop trading for revenge is how important is it to you? We have found that any change is possible, if it matters enough to the individual. Yes, you may have a type A personality and you may get upset and angry over market reversals, but that does not mean that you have to act in an angry manner as a trader. If it is important enough to you to begin to control your emotions when trading, you will.

Smitty is a typical trader who has experienced some ups and downs in his six years as an online trader. For the most part, Smitty has been able to make a decent living in the trading game although he admits to having had some "rather lean months" from time to time. Smitty is an extremely cyclical trader in that he goes through brief hot streaks followed by weeks of damaging losses. As a result, he has not reached the level of success that he had hoped to by now. He believes that the reason that he has not been able to get his trading game to the next level is because of his temper.

When Smitty came to our firm, it turned out that he was the perfect example of a trader who makes the mistake of going into the market and trading for revenge. When he is doing well, things are fine, but when he does poorly, things spin out of control and become horrendous.

SMITTY VERSUS THE MARKET

Trading Coach:	Hey Smitty, how is your month going?
Smitty:	Pretty awful. I am just going through one of my down times.
Trading Coach:	What do you mean "down times"?
Smitty:	Oh, you know, the typical slump. I think I have had one or two winning days in the past three weeks.
Trading Coach:	Wow! That must be tough. How are you handling it?
Smitty:	I guess ok, I'm pretty used to it by now because it happens every once in a while.
Trading Coach:	So this happens from time to time?
Smitty:	Yeah, I suppose.
Trading Coach:	Have you noticed any kind of pattern?
Smitty:	What do you mean?
Trading Coach:	Well, what I mean is do you find that the same things or feelings

	happen each time you start to go through these "down times"?
Smitty:	Yeah, I guess, kinda.
Trading Coach:	And?
Smitty:	Well, it's like this—I'll be going ok for a while and then things start to change—I'm not sure why or even what, but it's like I just look up and realize that I have not had a winner in a while.
Trading Coach:	Yeah . . .
Smitty:	Umm, it's hard to explain and I know this sounds crazy but it's like it gets to the point where every trade I make goes against me. I mean *every* trade.
Trading Coach:	No it does not sound crazy. It's actually pretty common among some traders. I know how frustrating that must be!
Smitty:	You have no idea. Frustrating to say the least. You see, I also have been known to have a . . . well . . . a bad temper.
Trading Coach:	Yeah . . .
Smitty:	It starts with me getting mad at myself for making such stupid trades and then I . . . uh . . . actually get ticked at the market until I eventually just kinda lose it.
Trading Coach:	And how does that affect your trading style?
Smitty:	I completely fall apart, but the

(continued)

worst part is I don't stop trading. I keep on trading. It's like I want to get back at the market for taking my money. By the time I'm done I have put myself into an even deeper hole and practically given back a month's worth of profits.

What Smitty is describing is the common experience that almost all traders go through at one time or another. Typically it begins with traders having a poor week or a very frustrating day. We are talking about one of those days when they are sticking to their game plan but things are just not going their way. But they keep on trading, trying to work their way through it thinking that they are just going through a minor slump. Eventually, nothing is going right and they begin to think,

"I can't believe it. What's with this market today? Every trade I make goes against me. It feels like the market knows whether I am short or long."

Then, they lose their discipline and succumb to their anger,

"That's it. I'll show this market what I can do. Now I'm going to get serious and start making my money back."

These traders have just spiraled into the abyss of trading for revenge.

While trading for revenge, traders oftentimes turn bad days into record-breaking losers by giving back their whole month (or even year) in one angered trading frenzy. As trading coaches, we have seen and heard of this situation occurring all too frequently. It is a sad phenomenon, but the almost comical part is that these traders are seeking revenge against a relentless, uncaring, unpredictable, uncontrollable enemy: the market. There is no way to get revenge against the market. But that is exactly what traders like Smitty are trying to do.

When competitive athletes feel that they have performed well but things are not going their way they sometimes become frustrated, begin to take their setbacks personally, and look for revenge. The following is a story about one of the greatest tennis players of all time, Arthur Ashe, and how his career nearly ended before it started because of his tendency to lose control.

EVOLUTION OF A CHAMPION

Arthur Ashe, two-time U.S. Amateur winner and the 1968 U.S. Open Champion, is perhaps best remembered for one of the most surprising upsets in tennis history—his 6–1, 6–1, 5–7, 6–4 demolition of reigning champion Jimmy Connors in the 1975 Wimbledon Men's Final. Connors had won both the U.S. Open and Wimbledon the previous year, and was a heavy favorite to defeat the flamboyant, but often erratic, Ashe in the final. But Ashe came out with a surprising game plan against the hard-hitting Connors, and he stuck with it throughout the four sets that it took to reach victory. Instead of matching his power against that of Connors, he played a disconcerting game of soft pushes, lobs, and dink shots. He would draw Connors to the net with a low, soft shot, and then lob it deftly over his

(continued)

opponent's head on the next shot. Faced with an opponent who refused to be drawn into a game of smashing power tennis, Connors became increasingly frustrated as the match wore on. He made a large number of uncharacteristic errors, and ended the match completely bewildered at the turn of events. An enduring image in sports is that of Ashe on the changeovers between games, sitting with a towel draped over his head as he blocked out the crowd and his opponent and focused on his own game plan. It worked, and Ashe became the first black Men's Wimbledon champion.

Arthur Ashe's victory is a testament to the power of the thinking game in sports because he did not overpower his opponent with technical superiority, he outthought and outstrategized him. It takes a cool head to prevail in such circumstances, and Ashe, who went on to become U.S. Davis Cup Captain, was one of the coolest in the game. But it was not always so. As a young tennis player growing up in Richmond, Virginia, Ashe describes himself as a hothead. Like many players today, he would get upset in games, yell, throw his racket, and argue points with his opponents. Then one day, his father, Arthur Ashe, Sr., came to see Arthur play. He was appalled at his son's disgraceful behavior, but he did not say anything until they got home. Then he took young Arthur's racket and locked it away, promising him that he would never see it again.

He explained to his son that as a young black man playing a game dominated by whites, he would not only have to always be on his best behavior, he would have to behave better than all the other players out there. He explained to his son that his critics would always be looking for a chance to disgrace him, and that angry outbursts such as the one he had witnessed that day would give others the perfect excuse to deny Ashe opportunities to play in the best tournaments. And so, he told his son, taking away his racket and ending his tennis career now was the best move he could make.

Arthur Ashe speaks of the next week as being the most miserable of his life. Since he had taken up the game at the age of seven after watching the accomplished black player, Ron Charity, working alone on his tennis serve at a public court in Richmond, tennis had been the love of Ashe's life. It was his passion, and the thought of having to do without it made him sick to his stomach. He sweated through the next week, hoping that his father would relent, terrified that he would not. His father was a strict man and a stern disciplinarian, and young Arthur had no way to judge how serious he was. Then, after a week, his father unlocked the cupboard and gave Arthur his racket back. But there was one condition. If Arthur ever threw another tantrum on the court, the racket would disappear permanently. Arthur Ashe kept his promise. Tennis meant that much to him.

How much does being a successful online trading athlete mean to you?

When athletes lose control, they run the risk of not being able to take their game to the next level. We call this pressing. The athlete is trying hard, almost too hard. In fact, what happens is that the more extra effort he or she exerts, the worse he or she seems to do. As Arthur Ashe's story illustrates, had he not learned how to play within himself when the pressure was on, he may never have defeated

Jimmy Connors and gone on to become one of the greatest tennis players of all time.

PRACTICE MAKES PERFECT, RIGHT?

Have you ever heard the saying "practice makes perfect"? This is sometimes a dangerous philosophy to live by. For all of us, especially traders, perfection is unobtainable, so training to be perfect can be a frustrating experience. If you train to be perfect you are simply setting yourself up for failure. We are human and make errors; remember, errors are not failures, but valuable learning experiences. The market can take the form of a volatile beast or a sleeping giant, but time has proven that it is impossible to predict consistently. So that leads us back to realizing what we can and cannot control and the reality is that there are only a limited number of things that we can control in competitive situations. Here again the trading athlete can learn from their sports counterparts.

In any game, a football player is faced with a daunting array of factors over which he has no control. For example, the weather, crowd noise, and umpire decisions can all influence the outcome of the game, but there is nothing the player can do about any of them. Other factors that he can influence but not really control include the play of his teammates, the coaches' decisions, and how well his opponents play.

As football players become more experienced, they learn not to pay attention to these peripheral factors. Instead, they learn to focus intently on the factors over which they have direct control:

- Maximizing effort on every play
- Executing the right play at the right time

- Blocking their assigned opponent
- Looking for the opportunity to make a big play

It is a player's individual ability to do these things well that makes all the difference in a team sport like football. A great football player is a master of concentration. He can filter through all the distractions and "lock in" or focus with laser-like accuracy on the critical factors over which he has control.

There are many similarities between the football player's situation and yours as a trading athlete. Once you push that button to make a trade it is out of your hands where your order gets filled. On a market order, you may end up paying more than you wanted or selling it at a lower price. These factors can be very frustrating, but if you have a solid game plan in place then you will realize that there is nothing more you can do about them because it is part of the trading game. The worst mistake you can make as a trader is to spend time and energy concentrating on such peripheral factors. Learn to avoid thinking about how much more money you would have made or how much less money you would have lost if the trade had been filled at a better price. The fact is you are filled at this price, you cannot change it, so you can only improve your performance by focusing on the factors that you can control, such as what your next trade will be, how many shares it will be, and when you are going to initiate it. Remember, just as with football players, what separates the starters from the benchwarmers is whether they accept the uncontrollable and remain focused on what they can control by concentrating on the truly important factors of the trading game.

Let us take another example from an individual sport. Imagine you are out playing a round of golf on the weekend. It is a great day, sunny and warm, and you are buoyed by the fact that you are actually shooting a pretty good score for a change. You come to the 15th hole and make a great drive down the center of the fairway. Whack! Look at that baby fly! No wind to slow it down or push it away, just straight, smooth sailing. Great job! Now you are left with about 150 yards to the pin and you have to clear a water hazard to reach the green. No big deal, right? Your swing is feeling smooth and solid so you select your club, go through your preshot routine, and swing away. Great contact. Looks like it is right on target. Wait a second, what is that? The head wind picks up and your ball seems to be hanging. Go, go, go, come on, make it—splash! What happens next will depend entirely on what sort of player you are.

If you have not learned to be a strong mental competitor, you will get upset that your shot did not have the desired result. This attitude is a recipe for disaster. Just as with the football player, the golfer can control only a limited number of factors on any shot. They can choose the club, control their tempo, execute the mechanics of their swing smoothly, but then they have to wait to see the outcome. They cannot control the wind or the bumpiness of a green, although they can try to make allowances for them. Part of the beauty of sports is that every game involves luck (does this remind you of trading?). By the way, ask any successful trader and they will tell you that they would rather be lucky than good.

The player who does not accept this part of the game will be upset by how unfairly their shot turned out. They might curse the wind, swear, or just stew inside, but the trouble is, they are still thinking about that last shot when they make their next. The result? They are not paying 100 percent attention on their next shot, and it will not be as good as it could have been if they were truly focused. If they allow themselves to get really upset, they may try to make a "miracle" shot, one they would never normally try, in order to "make up" for the shot that they were just "robbed" of. The player is trying to get revenge for their bad luck! In 90 percent or more of cases, a weekend golfer trying a miracle shot gets into even worse trouble than he or she was in before. The result is too often a disastrous score on the hole, instead of the acceptable bogey or double bogey that would have occurred if the player had stayed focused and made a high percentage shot after their misfortune.

If you are the type of competitor who has absorbed the lessons of this chapter, you can accept what has occurred, learn from it, and prepare for your next shot. Yes, you made a mistake, or you had some bad luck. Yes, it will cost you a shot. But if you leave the mistake behind and move on you will not compound the error by getting upset and allowing your anger and frustration to dictate your next shot. Even after a bad shot, many solid players can make a bogey or double bogey at worst, and this is just part of the game of golf. But very high scores are hard to recover from, and leave an ugly taste at the end of the round.

You can learn the same lessons and apply them to your everyday trading. Leave mistakes behind and move on. Focus on what is ahead of you; avoid looking back at what is behind you. Above all, avoid thinking that you have to prove yourself after making a mistake. Mistakes happen, and if you try to get revenge, you will get burned. The market has no personal feelings. It harbors no animosity toward you (despite how it might appear). If you allow yourself to start trading on the basis of your feelings, rather than on your analysis of the situation, you are beaten before you even begin.

Here are some of the common signs of trading for revenge. If any of these behaviors describe you, step back and think about your attitude. Are you trading to really be successful or do you only want to look successful? There is a big difference.

- Increasing the number of shares you trade as the result of trying to make your money back more quickly.

An example of this would be if you usually trade 500 to 1,000 shares per trade and then, out of the blue, start making trades of 3,000 shares each. Sure, sometimes you may get lucky and make a killing, but in the long run an all-star trader should only increase their share or position size when they are on the upswing and have established a successful trading pattern rather than as a careless effort to recoup losses.

- Increasing the number of trades you make on losing days. This is known as overtrading.
- Feelings of helplessness or giving up after a losing trade such as "I don't care what happens."
- Making a trade and then expecting it to be a loser or even hoping for it to be a loser so you can tell yourself, "See, I told you so."
- Comparing yourself to other online trading athletes and trying to keep up with them.
- Not thinking for yourself and just making trades based solely on suggestions by others or even making trades just because you saw someone else buy or sell something.

Now that you know what trading for revenge is and some of the signs to look for, how can you overcome it? Here are some very practical suggestions for dealing with the trading for revenge mentality. Our clients have successfully used these to overcome their own tendencies toward seeking revenge on the market, so these strategies are tried and true.

- Lower the size of your trades (from 500 or 1,000 shares per trade to 10 or 50 shares per trade) and start shooting from the hip. Go ahead, get it out of your system. And then when your trigger finger gets sore and you get tired of throwing away your hard-earned money, you can call a time-out and regain your composure. Now why do we recommend lowering your size of trades? Well, for two reasons. The first is so you do not blow out your account in a fit of rage (that would be kind of like going out, partying all night, and then waking up with a big tattoo of your name across your forehead). The second reason is so you can see how out of control you are capable of getting (the purpose of this is to provide you with a safe atmosphere—less than 50 shares—so you can take a careful look at your anger potential and learn from it).

- If this is not your style then you can simply get away from the computer. Throw your fit, walk around the room or outside, curse like a sailor (if it helps)—do whatever works for you. Trading is a competitive game, but remember whom you are competing against—yourself.

- Finally, you can just call it a day. The fact is that sometimes the other team is just on top of their game and there is nothing you can do about it. So tip your hat to the pitcher, call it a day, and focus on tomorrow's game. Perhaps the market has got you rattled—heck, perhaps the market has everyone spooked—and it may be much wiser to take a long time-out, regain composure and focus, and start fresh tomorrow.

As we have discussed, athletes often get caught up in destructive patterns by losing focus and trying too hard. For example, a pitcher who hangs a curve over the plate and then gives up a home run, oftentimes faces the next batter with anger rather than control. Naturally, what then happens is the floodgates open because he has lost his edge. Runs begin to pile up and before long, the pitcher has turned one bad pitch into eight hits and five earned runs.

All online trading athletes have either fallen into the trap of trading for revenge or been tempted to walk down that road at one time or another. Another effective strategy that can be used to help prevent you from trading for revenge is the use of a daily performance log.

Athletes often use logs to monitor their performance, provide themselves with feedback, and see if any patterns develop. As an online trading athlete, your log can provide you with some insight as to how many winning/losing days you tend to have per week, how many trades you tend to make, if they appear in groups, and what are your trading patterns. Once you have this information, you will be equipped to avoid trading for revenge.

An example of a two-week performance log is shown in Figure D.

Note: Good/bad trades should be determined by whether or not you stuck to your game plan, stayed in control, and remained disciplined, not by whether they were winners or losers.

COACH'S EVALUATION OF PERFORMANCE LOG

It is obvious that this online trading athlete is very "streaky" and probably does not have a solid grasp of their PTA (see Chapter 4). On the up days, this trader became tentative while on the down days, the trader lost site of his or her discipline and made three to four times more trades (overtrading), indicating a tendency toward falling into the trap of trading for revenge.

Oftentimes, a successful online trading athlete will make a good trade that does not turn out to be profitable. In other words, they stuck to their game plan, properly researched

FIGURE D   WEEKLY PERFORMANCE LOG

Day	UP/ DOWN $	Good Trades	Bad Trades	Total Trades	Comments
Monday	down	8	44	52	Lost focus in morning and made some rookie mistakes, gotta stop overtrading!
Tuesday	up	7	3	10	Made big money on first trade of the day!
Wednesday	up	10	2	12	I am feeling great, made some awesome trades today! Keep it going.
Thursday	up	11	4	15	Had bad morning but came back strong in the afternoon.
Friday	down	6	24	30	I felt like I was pressing, I need to be more patient and relax.
Monday	down	4	28	32	I just couldn't find my rhythm all day, and ended up overtrading.
Tuesday	down	3	37	40	Had another bad day, starting to lose confidence, I need to slow it down a bit.
Wednesday	up	4	2	6	Better day than past couple, cut down on my size and trades.
Thursday	down	2	18	20	Had trouble getting any momentum, still felt a little tentative.
Friday	up	6	0	6	Another big day, I really needed it, got lucky in the morning.

Overall Evaluation:

I am having trouble staying consistent. I took a really big hit on Monday and Tuesday but was able to save my week with Friday's trade at the open. I'm still getting frustrated and overtrading when I'm down. I need to work on staying relaxed and focused especially when things go against me.

the trade, and made a confident, calculated decision. Unfortunately, the market went against them, for no apparent reason (just like the wind picking up in our golf example), and the end result was a money losing trade. This does not mean that the trader made a bad trade (or that the golfer made bad shot); it simply means that there were factors outside of his or her control and that is just part of the game.

This is similar to a hitter who makes solid contact every at-bat, but the players in the field make great plays. The hitter was successful in his at-bat even though he did not reach base safely. As a result, a hitter with a positive mental attitude will see this as going 4 for 4, rather than 0 for 4 because he is counting quality at-bats as the method of evaluating his level of performance. The bottom line is that in the long run, this batter will experience fewer slumps and achieve more consistent success.

Just as a baseball player can interpret his performance in a different light, online trading athletes can evaluate their level of performance in a similar manner by reviewing their trading log and counting the number of good trades they had compared to the number of bad (undisciplined) trades they made.

A great addition to your trading log would be to evaluate each trade you make as you make it. This is a fantastic strategy for new traders or slumping traders because they will be able to evaluate their performance as it occurs. Make sure and write down notes next to the trades (what you did right/wrong, what were your reasons for making the trade, would you make the trade again if the same situation occurred). This will provide you with a blow-by-blow analysis of your trading performance so that you can learn from your strengths and restructure your weaknesses.

As we wind down this chapter we want to tell you a short story about a former client of ours named Richard. We think this story highlights a majority of the concepts that we discussed throughout this chapter.

Richard was in his mid-40s and going through his third career change. He was well educated and had spent more than 20 years in the financial world where he had worked his way up through the financial hierarchy and he had a great job as an analyst for a major brokerage firm. After years of doing this, he felt like he was getting a little stale so he decided to give notice and venture into the world of online trading. After all, he was a successful analyst and had handled some major accounts throughout his career so how different could it be? Well, Richard quickly found out how different it really was.

He was not getting filled where he wanted, he could not get out of trades when he wanted, and he was even getting margin calls every so often because he kept on forgetting that he was now dealing with his personal account rather than his corporate cash reserves. Richard was struggling and beginning to doubt his decision to transition into the online trading game. The part that was eating him up was that he understood the market as well as anyone. He was an expert in charting theory and interpreting economic data so what was the problem? Months went by and Richard was losing money—big money. He had blown through his account in the first month after some bad trades so he was now dipping into his savings to try to make a comeback. The longer he went, the more frustrated he became, and the lower his confidence level dropped. He was being swallowed up by the market. The day finally came when he realized that he was in over his head so he began to send out resumes to return to his previous (unexciting but stable) job as an analyst. As he was waiting for interview calls, he figured he might as well still dabble in the market. As luck would have it, and unbeknownst to anyone else, Richard was about to become a part of the dot-com frenzy.

Now that Richard was back on his feet, replenishing his savings, and turning huge profits, he decided that he did not want to make the same mistake twice. He knew that his turnaround was due to luck. He had no illusion that he had become a master online trader overnight—he knew that he was just in the right place at the right time and with the right position on.

Because of his self-awareness, he decided to contact our firm for some coaching so that he could fully understand

Trading Coach:	Did you ever play any competitive sports in high school or college?
Richard:	Yeah, sure. Some basketball, football, and baseball.
Trading Coach:	Which was your best sport?
Richard:	Probably baseball.
Trading Coach:	Ok, now we're getting somewhere. Were you a hitter or a pitcher?
Richard:	Hitter.
Trading Coach:	Great. Were you any good?
Richard:	I batted around .380 in college and made the all-conference team my junior and senior years.
Trading Coach:	Pretty impressive. I had trouble batting my weight in college. Never could hit that slider!
(We both laugh)	
Trading Coach:	Tell me this. When you were hitting what were you thinking about?
(Long pause)	
Richard:	Heck, I don't know. Nothing, really.
Trading Coach:	Exactly!

what it was that caused him to nearly self-destruct. One of our strategies when working with clients is to identify their natural strengths and help them parallel their experiences as a trader with their previous experiences as a competitor.

As Richard's story clearly shows, oftentimes, obstacles that traders face originate because they are thinking too much. In Richard's case, he was an analyst who was trying to transform into a day trader overnight. He was pressing. He was trying to control every aspect of every trade rather than focusing on his performance, trusting his abilities, and letting the trade run its course. In essence, we helped Richard understand that the reason he was a successful hitter was because he did not think—he trusted his abilities and reacted. With this in mind, he could achieve his potential as a trader if he played it with the same intensity and discipline that he used when playing baseball.

---◆---

TRADING FOR REVENGE: A RECIPE FOR DISASTER

- Factors we cannot control
  — Other traders
  — The market
  — The productivity of each company we trade

- Factors we can control
  — Maximizing effort on every trade
  — Executing the right trade at the right time
  — Looking for the opportunity to make a great trade

- How mistakes arouse anger

- The dangers of angry trading

- Warning signs of trading for revenge

- Keeping a performance log

CHAPTER SEVEN

RECOVERY FROM TRADING INJURIES: OVERCOMING FEAR

In the 2000 women's college basketball season, University of Connecticut star guard Shea Ralph experienced the ultimate sports joy when her team won the national championship with a rout of their arch-rival, the University of Tennessee. Few athletes have had to climb as many mountains as Shea Ralph did before she was able to taste the thrill of victory. As a freshman sensation on the Huskie team, she had been expected to help guide Connecticut to a national championship in 1998, but her season ended dramatically when she suffered a major knee injury in the final game before the playoffs. After surgery and six months of excruciating rehabilitation, Ralph came back to the game she loved, ready to lead another charge at the summit, only to see her 1999 season vanish when she injured the same knee again and again had to endure anterior cruciate ligament surgery.

Shea Ralph would have been forgiven if she had decided then and there to quit basketball and pursue safer, less painful activities. Not only did she face the prospect of enduring another bout of rehabilitation to get back in shape to play basketball, but also, there was no guarantee that she could ever play at the same level again. Two surgeries on the same knee cast doubt on her future. Would her doubly reconstructed knee be able to hold up to the pounding that goes along with a full college basketball season? Would she lose a step from her trademark quickness? Such questions hovered over her as she began the 2000 season.

Every day, thousands of athletes at the professional and college level have to face the same questions that Shea Ralph did. All competitive athletes must deal with injuries at some point during their career because injuries are an inherent part of competition. In their quest to be better than their opponents, modern athletes must train longer and harder, and push their performances closer to the edge than their predecessors ever did. Injuries are an inevitable byproduct of this intense level of training and competition, which has begun to filter down to even the high school level. Overcoming an injury involves overcoming pain and uncertainty, but also means facing and conquering fear and self-doubt. Although Shea Ralph overcame her successive injuries and led her Huskies to a national championship, other athletes are overcome by their fears and quit their sport or are never again able to play at the level that they once did.

Similarly, as an online trading athlete you are going to experience trading "injuries" on a reoccurring basis and how you deal with them will make or break your trading career. No, we are not talking about a physical injury like a pulled hamstring or sprained ankle or even carpal tunnel syndrome. What we are talking about are the trading injuries of sudden losses, unexpected poor performance of your stocks, market fluctuations that go against you, and similar crises that are impossible to predict and difficult to overcome. They can keep you out of the game for a while or, in extreme cases, force you into early retirement. In the previous chapter we described at length one typical response to such setbacks, the trading for revenge syndrome. This response is caused by feelings of anger and frustration. But market setbacks can also cause doubts and fears, the same sorts of self-doubts about one's ability that athletes such as Shea Ralph must face. Anxiety and self-doubt cause problems for online trading athletes, and require a different set of strategies and skills to overcome. In this chapter we discuss how to deal with the various "injuries" of trading and show you how to face your fears, overcome them, and move forward with success and enthusiasm.

AN INJURY HAPPENS ON THE ONLINE TRADING FIELD

You are in the market, having a pretty good day—not setting any records but content with how things are going. You have been watching the pharmaceutical sector for a while and have a couple of long positions that you have been accumulating. There is 150,000 on the bid and a couple of thousand at the offer. You keep on checking your indicators making sure everything is in line. You start to feel pretty confident, not mind reading-confident but as if you know what you are doing and have earned your spot in the starting lineup. You can almost smell the money you are going to make on this trade. You are even beginning to think that you are getting the hang of this game. What used to be a fast, confusing blur of lights and colors is now starting to become clear and make sense. You are seeing things that you did not even know existed not too long ago. All that hard work has paid off. Finally you are going to start to come into your own. Instead of sitting around watching everyone else make money, you are the one about whom they will be saying, "Man, he's on fire!"

As you sit back and enjoy your success for a moment you feel comfortable and confident. You are in the flow. But suddenly, the situation changes completely. Your mind races as you struggle to keep up with what is happening. "What on earth just happened? What's going on? This is no good, I can't let this happen. There was supposed to be support at that level!"

The whistle blows! Time-out. Bring out the stretcher, there's an injury on the field.

After the injury

The critical aspect of a trading injury is not the event itself but your reaction to the event. Athletes know that even if they stay in great shape and take good care of themselves, there is no way to prevent an unexpected injury. Sometimes it is just bad luck. Online trading athletes must realize this also. Despite the best precautions and despite sticking to a well-developed system, sometimes you get blindsided. After such a trading injury, it is only natural to experience anxiety. The trader wonders if he or she somehow made a terrible mistake, if he or she really belongs in the business, and if more problems are likely to occur. The problem with this reaction is that it makes traders tentative. They approach future trades hesitantly and without confidence. They miss their usual trading opportunities. And often, when they sense trouble, they back out of positions or minimize exposure, minimizing possible profits as well. The following story about Heather, a former client of ours, illustrates how a trading injury can directly impact an online trading athlete's performance.

HESITANT HEATHER

Heather has been trading for a year but still has not developed any real consistency in her trading game. She admits that the first four months were awful and that she was not sure whether she had made the right choice to try to learn how to trade. After her first four months, she began to take in some profits, nothing big, but at least she was gaining some confidence in her ability. Unfortunately, her success was temporary and she began to become extremely erratic in her trading performance. She would have good days followed by several bad days; it got to the point where she felt like she was back where she started from nine months ago. Lost, confused, and frustrated, she contacted us to see if we could help.

COMING BACK FROM DISASTER

Trading Coach:	Hey, Heather. So tell me what's been going on.
Heather:	Where should I start? I guess, I just don't know if I am cut out for this trading thing.
Trading Coach:	What makes you think that?
Heather:	Well, every time I think that I am getting the hang of this, I have two or three bad days in a row. I'm pretty fed up with the whole thing, really.
Trading Coach:	I see . . . You said "bad days." Could you describe a typical one for me?

(continued)

Heather:	Yeah, I guess. Uh, well, let's see, I guess it starts with my first couple of trades in the day. I mean, I don't trade big at all, only about 200 to 400 shares at a time. Anyway, I'll be watching the bid/ask, you know stuff like whose coming in, whose getting out, which side market makers are on ... things like that, just trying to get a feel for it.
Trading Coach:	Yeah ...
Heather:	Well, and then I'll finally enter into a position that I feel pretty comfortable with, although I'll admit it does take me some time to commit to it, but that way at least I know I've done my research on it and I am not rushing into it. So I usually feel pretty good about it.
Trading Coach:	It sounds like you feel confident with that approach.
Heather:	Oh, I do—it just takes me a little longer to get into a trade.
Trading Coach:	So what happens next?
Heather:	Um ... I'll be in the trade and then it sometimes goes a little against me. I don't immediately hit the panic button, although I used to but I stopped doing that, I just kinda reevaluate what's going on.
Trading Coach:	Sounds good. What next?
Heather:	Well, if the trade does not start to come back in a couple of minutes, I

	start to feel really nervous. I begin to get this weird feeling in my feet. I know it's weird but that's what happens.
Trading Coach:	It's actually not weird at all, in fact, it's pretty normal. So when you start to get nervous what do you then do?
Heather:	To be honest, I usually close the position out for a loss. I just can't seem to tolerate the feeling of not knowing what is going to happen and possibly taking a big loss.
Trading Coach:	That's interesting, because for the most part, online trading is all about never knowing what is going to happen.
Heather:	Yeah, I know. And I know that I have to stop doing this or I'll never get any good at trading.
Trading Coach:	Can you think back to when you first noticed this happening to you?
Heather:	I'm not sure, but I think it was two or three months ago, right when I started to make a little money.
Trading Coach:	Do you keep copies of your time and sales or a trading log?
Heather:	I don't keep my time and sales from that long ago, but I do keep a pretty good trading log.
Coach:	Would you mind if I took a look at it?
Heather:	No, not at all.

(continued)

Trading Coach:	Great, ok, let's see ... Yeah, it looks like you started to have some winners back here. You were doing ok.
Heather:	Yeah, I guess.
Trading Coach:	Hey what's this? That's a pretty big loss for you. Do you remember what happened?
Heather:	Oh, yeah, how could I forget? That was the biggest loss I've had so far. It was pretty dumb of me, you know. I was just starting to make some money and I decided to bump up my size so I could do even better. I was long 400 shares and the stock just started to move up a bit so I bought 400 more—to be long a total of 800 shares, the biggest position I have ever had. And then out of nowhere, the stock just dropped. At first, I froze and then I tried to get out but I was not getting filled—there must have been a bunch of sell orders in front of me. That was the *worst!* I ended up losing my whole week on that one trade. Anyway, when I finally got out, I stopped trading for the day and decided to take the next day off from trading so I could sort out what happened.
Trading Coach:	That sounds like a good idea. And were you able to sort things out?
Heather:	Yeah, the best I could but it just was not the same after that. I started

being overcautious and was passing
up on trades that I would have made
the previous week.

Trading Coach: Sounds like you may still be dealing
with what we call a trading injury.

As a result of experiencing a trading injury, Heather became hesitant, nervous, and fearful. Her progress as a trader
had essentially been halted and had even regressed in some
respects, because she never fully recovered from the injury.
In order to help traders like Heather get back into the
game, we teach them how to deal with their fears, overcome
their anxiety, and recover from their trading injury.

Let us look at anxiety and see what it really is, how it de-
velops, and what can be done about it.

WHAT IS ANXIETY?

Anxiety is a natural response to a threat or challenge. If you
do not think you can successfully meet the challenge you are
faced with, you are likely to experience anxiety. What you
think about the challenge is most important. Anxiety is not
caused by the situation itself, but by your attitude toward the
situation. Anxiety affects everyone in two ways: it impacts
our thoughts and our feelings.

THOUGHTS

When anxiety strikes, your mind becomes full of unwanted
thoughts. These thoughts take up most of your attention
and make it hard for you to concentrate on anything else.
"What was I doing in that position, I'll never make back that

trade. Why did I do something so stupid?" With thoughts like these, it is impossible to be relaxed and confident.

FEELINGS

The physical feelings of anxiety are unpleasant, and most people do their best to avoid them. These include difficulty or changes in breathing; rapid or irregular heartbeat; nausea or discomfort in the stomach; muscle tension; cold skin; increased sweat; dizziness; and/or a numb feeling in certain body parts.

There are two main stages to anxiety. The first stage of anxiety is nervousness. This comes from anticipating a threat or challenge. The competitive athlete thinks about the playoff game on the weekend, and just the thought of it gives him sweaty palms and a queasy stomach. The online trading athlete imagines the market suddenly moving against his current position and his heart races and his blood pressure rises. This nervousness is a perfectly natural part of competition for both athletes and traders, but it can make some people very uncomfortable.

The second stage of anxiety is panic. Success is impossible in this stage. Characteristics of a state of panic include:

- You freeze up when you are long and you see a large sell order come into the market.
- You cannot focus because your mind begins to race through "what if" scenarios.
- You feel out of control and begin to hit the panic button, throwing your game plan out the window.
- You dig yourself into a deeper hole because you are confused and are trying to find a quick solution to the situation.

All of these reactions can hinder performance. While nervousness is a normal reaction to the challenge of trading or competing, panic is never desirable.

Even a single trading injury can cause an online trading athlete to associate feelings of anxiety with similar trading situations. A series of injuries makes it even more likely that these feelings will occur. As a result, the online trading athlete may begin to avoid such situations because they do not want to experience anxiety. It is impossible to be an excellent trader if there are some situations that you always avoid.

CHOKING

Another consequence of anxiety is what athletes call choking. When athletes choke, their anxiety levels overwhelm their coping responses and they experience high levels of tension that prevent them from achieving their peak performance. An example of this would be a quarterback in a football game who has been sacked several times and no longer feels confident enough to stay in the pocket. Online trading athletes who choke will be so tense and distracted that they will fail to recognize the signals they should be watching for and will make poor trades.

BURNOUT

Finally, anyone who experiences anxiety for an extended period of time is likely to suffer from burnout. For example, a pro golfer who becomes so anxious about his short game that he worries about it all day and stops enjoying or looking forward to golfing tournaments is more likely to drop out of the tour in an attempt to get rid of the anxiety. The same can be true of online trading athletes who feel so anxious about their trading activity that they dread the start of each trading day, and look forward only to the closing bell when they can get away from it all.

Successful online trading athletes are consistently able to deal with the normal feelings of nervousness and prevent panic from impacting their performance

LEARN HOW TO RELAX WHEN ANXIOUS

We all know that anxiety interferes with effective performance, no matter what the competitive situation. You must recognize that it is normal to get nervous when you are anticipating a challenge, such as right before economic data are released. Some people will tell you they do not get nervous before big events, but these folks are either the exception or simply unwilling to admit the truth. If you are like the rest of us and you get nervous before a big event, you need to tap into it and welcome it as a positive indicator. It might seem awkward at first, but if you are willing to put some practice time in, you will realize that your nervousness can become a strong asset and help you win the mental part of the game. When properly channeled, nervousness can help you concentrate more sharply, increase your reaction speed, and even energize you when you need it. Here is an example of some self-talk that you can use when you get that anxious feeling. Take a second to adapt it to fit your specific trading situation.

I'm nervous, that's good. I'm prepared for this earnings report and I'm ready to go. I'm excited. Bring it on.

How to Prevent Panic

Nervousness will not hurt your performance, but panic will. What do you do if you start to feel overwhelmed by your anxious thoughts and feelings? Relaxation skills are very helpful at this stage. The only way out of a mess is to calm down and not panic. When your heart starts to race or your stomach begins to twist in knots, a relaxation exercise can get rid of these feelings and help you stay focused on your trading positions. If you practice relaxation exercises on a regular basis, you will be ready to use them when you really need them.

Professional athletes and online trading athletes do not have a lot of time to respond to the challenges that are thrown at them. In the middle of a busy day, if the market suddenly starts to move wildly, with lots of asynchrony between sectors, you may only have moments to make some critical decisions. This is not much different than a quarterback who is facing third and eight on his own 15-yard line and only has split seconds to decide on a play and to spot the open receiver. If he hesitates too long, a rampaging linebacker may blindside him for a disastrous sack. In such situations, it is natural to become flustered and make a mistake. Instead, this is the moment when you most need to respond effectively.

Knowing a simple relaxation strategy very well will help you master these unexpected challenges. One-breath relaxation or centering are both good techniques to use at such times. In Appendix A, Part I, we go over a number of different relaxation strategies together. Some of these you will find very helpful, and they will become an important part of your coping strategies. Others may not suit your own particular style, and that is all right. We only ask that you try each method at least once to see how it works for you.

QUICKLY RECOVERING FROM A TRADING INJURY

What can you do as an online trading athlete to quickly recover from the inevitable trading injuries you will experience in your career?

Here are eight suggestions that will help you deal with the injuries of trading.

1. Next time you experience a trading injury, maintain your discipline by closing your position (or at least put some stop orders in) and calling a time-out.
2. Now, examine your feelings. Are you upset and angry? Shaken and scared? Confused and doubtful? Now is the time to begin to confront and process the injury.
3. Try to calm down using a relaxation strategy. Choose your favorite and best strategy to relax. Use it immediately. If it is deep breathing, take some of those deep, refreshing breaths. If it is centering, stand up and find your calm center.
4. Now begin to evaluate the situation. By taking the time right now, when a trading injury happens, to learn from it and work your way through it, you will save money in the future. We have said it before, and we will say it again, successful trading is more about limiting your losses than collecting winners.

5. Write down the current date and time, number of shares you had, whether you were long or short, size of bid and offer before the injury, what market makers were involved, and any other indicators or factors that you can remember.

6. Next, write down your emotions. How did you feel before the injury occurred? How did you feel afterward? Did your relaxation strategy help? Why or why not? Every problem situation is a potential learning experience for the online trading athlete with a positive trading attitude (PTA) (see Chapter 4). You can stay a step ahead of other traders by learning from a bad experience.

7. Now accept the fact that the situation was out of your control. Write it down: "The market turning was out of my control and I am ok with that. That is the way the game is played. I have survived previous injuries and will make it through this one." Do some more relaxation in order to get ready to start again.

8. Now let us put our helmet back on and get our confidence back. To do this, put your shoulders back, keep your head up, take one or two cleansing breaths and write down some of your natural strengths such as how talented, successful, good looking, well dressed, whatever you want. The truth is, it really does not matter what you compliment yourself on as along as you are complimenting (rather than criticizing) yourself. "I am an online trading athlete and injuries are part of the game. I am a competitor and survivor. I am in control of myself . . . And boy do I feel sexy!"

Now that you have worked your way through these steps, the last thing you need to do is smile, tell yourself it is game time and get back on the field.

Wait a minute: sexy? What are you talking about? Let us tell you a story about an elite baseball player we once worked with not too long ago, who we will refer to as Stan. Stan was a 6-foot 4-inch, 245-pound rock-solid outfielder who was not exactly born with movie-star good looks. Throughout his exceptional college career, he was a nation-leading power hitter and had scouts drooling over him until he became eligible for the draft. Now try to understand, this was a ballplayer who was consistently at the top of his game, season after season. So, one day we asked him, "What separates you from other power hitters? How are you able to maintain that intensity level even when you experience a hitting slump?" He looked at us and said point blank, "It does not matter whether I am 4 for 4 with four home runs or 0 for 4 with four strikeouts, every time I walk up to the plate, I tell myself that I feel sexy!"

What surprised us was not that he said that to himself, but that he actually believed it! Needless to say we all had a good laugh over his choice of self-talk and confidence-building strategy but the point is it worked for him and that is all that mattered. Today he is still feeling sexy every time he steps up to the plate as he continues to be successful in his professional baseball career.

SUMMARY

Injuries are an unavoidable part of life, both for the elite athlete and for the online trading athlete. A basketball player may be driving to the net, collide with a defender in the lane and ends up blowing out his knee; a hitter may get beaned in the face with a fastball; a wide receiver who goes over the middle for a catch may end up getting laid out by the middle linebacker. In each of these cases, the athlete experiences a significant amount of trauma. How well they recover from this trauma will help determine their future career. For the online trading athlete, this same experience can be had when the market runs you over and you just happen to have more exposure than you normally do such as the first time you bump up the size of your trades from 100 shares to 1,000 shares or from 1,000 shares to 5,000 shares. Sure enough, you get clobbered. But what will make you a long-term success as a trader is how you respond to this setback.

If the athlete experiences fear in similar situations, then he or she is likely to avoid future situations related to that event even after he or she has physically healed from the injury. An example of this is when the basketball player physically recovers from the knee injury but is unable to drive to the net in a game. As a result, the basketball player avoids the situation in the game and performance suffers. The basketball player ends up being caught in a circular pattern of fear and avoidance, which prevents him or her from ever reaching his or her potential (see Figure E).

The same is true for online trading athletes who get burned in the market. They become tentative and remain

FIGURE E TRADING INJURY MODEL

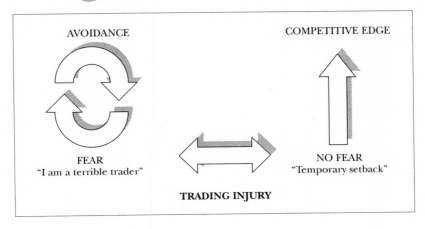

AVOIDANCE

COMPETITIVE EDGE

FEAR
"I am a terrible trader"

NO FEAR
"Temporary setback"

TRADING INJURY

stuck in the fear-avoidance pattern, which results in dwindling returns and stagnation at best. In essence, online trading athletes who experience fear have lost their competitive edge.

Successful competitors view injuries as temporary setbacks rather than permanent conditions and they accept them as a natural part of the trading game. Oftentimes, we have had online trading athletes tell us that they do not mind experiencing an injury once in a while because it keeps them sharp and on their toes. They do not want to experience them but they are able to stare the injuries right in the face and persevere, maintaining their competitive edge. In the trading game, the cliché, "What does not kill you, only makes you stronger" is accurate.

It is important to realize that effectively coping with trading injuries is a skill that can be learned. Please remember that coping is not just about you dealing with an injury alone. As an online trading athlete, you have coping resources available to you that you may not even be aware of. Have you ever had a bad day in the market and then you go online to a chat room or send an e-mail and vent your frustrations? Well that is using your peers as a coping resource. How about telling your friends, family, or significant other about it? Well, that is using relationships as a coping resource. How about getting in your car and going for a drive, or exercising, or eating, or watching television, or playing a video game, or reading a book? All of these are quality coping resources that online trading athletes use to deal with the injuries they experience in the trading game.

Here are some reactions to a trading injury that indicate poor coping. If any of these reactions describe you, you will need to work doubly hard on developing better skills for handling setbacks.

- Internalizing your anger: getting angry at yourself, calling yourself stupid
- Withdrawing from friends or family
- Moping around feeling sorry for yourself
- Repeatedly avoiding what you should be doing by doing something "more important" such as reading the newspaper, looking up a stock report, responding to e-mail

If you find that you often get anxious during your trading workday and the relaxation skills you have learned here do not seem to help, it may be time to ask yourself if you are in the right profession. Not everyone is cut out to be an online trading athlete just as not every athlete is cut out to play every position. For example, consider a football player. Sure, you could force a 6-foot 1-inch, 165-pound player to be a nose tackle but is that the best position for him? Probably not: from his description he sounds more like he a wide receiver or a defensive back. In much the same way, online trading athletes should evaluate their own personality type to determine what type of trading they are best equipped to do. Swing trader, position trader, momentum trader? The reality is that if you do not function well under constant pressure, then day trading may not be the best choice for you. You can still be a successful trader but you will need to learn to tap into your strengths.

Online trading athletes go through a number of trading injuries on a daily basis. It can wear you down, attack your ego, and lessen your confidence. If you allow trading injuries to take control of you, you have effectively thrown in the towel and forfeited your game. As an online trading athlete, you are smarter than that, so accept the injuries as they come. Face them head on, and use the relaxation and coping skills we have shown you to overcome your fears and anxieties and move ahead to a successful career.

—————————◆—————————

RECOVERY FROM TRADING INJURIES: OVERCOMING FEAR

- Injuries in the online trading game
- Common reactions to trading injuries
    — Anxiety
    — Thoughts
    — Feelings

- Stages of anxiety
    — Nervousness
    — Panic

- Learn how to relax when anxious
- How to prevent panic
- Relaxation strategies

CHAPTER EIGHT

CONCENTRATION: TUNING IN TO SUCCESS

Imagine that you have been invited by some business associates to play a round of golf at a great private club. Your group is next on the tee. There are about 15 or 16 people standing around waiting for you to tee off. What is going through your mind? If you are like many occasional golfers, your thoughts might go something like this. "Ok, no pressure. I just need to hit a good shot off the tee. I just don't want to top it like I usually do on the first tee. What if I don't make it past the ladies' tee box? How embarrassing! I should have taken some more swings on the driving range. My first tee is always my worst. Maybe someone else in my group will hit a bad tee shot so I won't feel so stupid if I miss my shot. Oh boy, everyone is hitting it right down the middle. Huh, oh, I'm up? Ok, whatever you do, don't duff this ball. Get ready. I wish those guys over there would stop talking. Look at the ball. One practice swing. Feels ok. Don't mess this one up. Hit it good. Oh, darn!" The ball squirts off the tee box into some thick bushes some 20 yards ahead and to the right. You did it again.

If this has ever happened to you, you are not alone. Sometimes we get so distracted by our own thoughts and nervousness that we lose concentration on the task at hand. To be a consistently successful athlete or online trading athlete, you need to be able to maintain your concentration under a variety of distracting conditions. Everyday distractions can affect your level of concentration and cause your performance to suffer. In the above example, you were talking yourself through your routine. The fact that you even knew that there were a lot of people watching you tee off, not to mention that you actually heard people talking right before you approached the ball, tells us that you had lost your concentration and were in trouble. Without the ability to screen out distractions and focus on the critical factors necessary for high-level performance, you will not be able to achieve success.

As an online trading athlete, there are an infinite number of factors that can distract you and cause you to lose your concentration: telephone calls; being hungry, tired, interrupted; e-mail; being uncomfortable in your chair; the list goes on. When athletes lose concentration, they make mistakes. The tennis player serves a double fault; the field goal kicker hits it wide right; the baseball player strikes out looking; the golfer swings and misses. What happens when you are in the game and lose concentration? You end up making poor trades. In this chapter, let us take a closer look at concentration and go over some strategies that can help you maintain focus, even in the face of distractions.

TUNING IN INSTEAD OF BLOCKING OUT

Athletes are often told to "block out" distractions by well-meaning coaches in order to stay focused. There are two problems with this. First, coaches rarely tell an athlete how to block out the distraction. Second, it is nearly impossible to intentionally block out all distractions, especially after we have become aware of them.

Take a basketball player, for example, who gets sent to the foul line for two free throws. The score is tied, there are 15 seconds on the clock, it is a real pressure situation. As we watch the game, what do we see happening behind the basket? A whole section of fans is waving balloons and screaming, trying to distract the athlete from making the free throw. The player has been told since he was about five years old to block out the distractions. Come on! Who are we kidding? There are so many different distractions going on that it is impossible to know where to begin. Should he block out the cheering fans behind the basket? His opponents glaring at him on either side of the lane? The scoreboard showing the tie score? The music pumping out from the loudspeakers? The referee standing behind him? The coaches yelling on the sidelines? Instead of being told to block out these things, the athlete should have been told to tune in on the shot.

Let us try a little experiment, ok? The instructions are simple. We will ask you a question and we want you to answer it with the first image that comes into your mind. Ready? Here we go.

Think of an animal but do *not* think of a hairy gorilla wearing a pink tutu. What animal are you thinking of?

Most likely you are currently thinking of hairy gorillas or at best fighting to think of an animal, any animal, that is not a hairy gorilla wearing a pink tutu. How is that for concentration? You only had to block out one thing and that is what you focused on! Way to go!

We are just giving you a hard time. The truth is that it is completely normal and natural to think of hairy gorillas wearing pink tutus in this situation. It is normal to think about anything once it has been introduced into your mind. How easy was it to block out the image of a hairy gorilla after it was suggested to you? If you gave yourself time to struggle with this task, you might have noticed that as long as you were trying to block out the hairy gorilla, you ended up thinking of a hairy gorilla. Most likely it was only after you started thinking about another animal (a pink elephant perhaps?) that you were able to get your mind off the hairy gorillas wearing tutus. Keep in mind that all we did was introduce one distraction to you. Now imagine how useless those earlier instructions to block out the distractions—all 1,000 of them—were to our young basketball player as he stood waiting to shoot his free throws!

The coach obviously means well and is trying to get his players to perform to their potential. Unfortunately, the coach is approaching concentration all wrong. You see, we perform better on skills when we tune in rather than block out. Every essential skill we have ever learned—writing, reading, typing, driving, and so on, involves far more tuning in than blocking out. For example, when you learned how to drive, you did not learn to block out all distractions. If you had, you would have ended up running red lights and crashing into trees and other vehicles. Actually, you learned what the important factors to pay attention to were and to focus on them while you were driving, allowing other, non-important factors to fade into the periphery.

Through experience, we usually learn to sort out what is important from what is not. Every experience, even a failure, is a learning experience. With experience, situations that at first seem confusing and hopeless become orderly and predictable. Even experts often do not realize how much they have learned from their performance experiences. Professor Bruce Abernathy, head of the Department of Movement Studies at Queensland University in Australia, found this to be true when he studied the reactions of the world's top squash players. He wanted to know why the best players were able to react so quickly to their opponent's serve. Contrary to what he expected, Abernathy found that the best players did not have faster reaction times. Testing showed that their reaction times were the same as less experienced players. Instead, he discovered that the best players could successfully predict where the squash ball was going to land before it had even been served. Although the players could not tell him how they did this, Abernathy found that the top players had learned to read the upper body movements of their opponents. By concentrating on cues provided by their opponent's arms and upper bodies, they gained crucial extra time to prepare for the serve. Less experienced players, however, concentrated on the cues provided by the wrist and racket movements of their opponents. Because these movements occur later in the process of serving, they could not react as quickly to the serve.

This is not much different from the successful online trading athlete's ability to focus in on the subtle, relevant signals they are able to detect from the market that will help them make a confident, quality trade. In contrast, rookie online trading athletes may easily become distracted by the noise, flashing lights, or irrelevant information on the screen thereby causing them to make a hasty, poor trade.

TUNED IN TERESA

Teresa has been an online trading athlete for six years. Like all successful competitors, she is consistently at the top of her game. Sure, she might occasionally take a hit in the market but any time that happens she is able to isolate the incident, regain her composure, and find her way through it. She has successfully become one of the few trading elite and she believes that it is because she has learned to filter through the distractions and focus in on her trades.

Trading Coach:	Hey Teresa, tell me what it's like to go into the market and know that you are going to be successful.
Teresa:	It's not about knowing I am going to make money, it's more like just feeling it. It's hard to explain. It's more like something that comes from within—that is part of me.
Trading Coach:	Do you feel like that every day?
Teresa:	Almost every day, really ... I mean, yeah, there are days when I feel sort of off, like my timing is off but I think the key is that I am at the point now where I can tune into that immediately and adjust my daily trading goals. And then I am able to slow things down a bit until I recover that feeling.
Trading Coach:	Were you always like that? I mean were you one of those traders who stepped right in and were successful?
Teresa:	Far from it! I was one of those traders who *thought* I could come right in and be successful, but soon ended up being shown the door and being told not to let it hit me in the butt as I left. I'll be honest, it took a while to learn the trading game but I worked hard at it and had a few lucky breaks along the way.
Trading Coach:	You said you "worked hard at it." What was the most important thing you think you had to work hard at?

Teresa:	That's easy, definitely not being suckered into the market and falling for those fake-outs. You know like when you take a position and then it immediately goes against you so you get out because you think you are wrong. I'll never forget those days. You just end up getting chewed up by the market makers. They are ruthless, heck no one cares if you go bankrupt. It's a lonely way to make a living. But in my opinion there is nothing like it. You either love it or hate it. And I love it.
Trading Coach:	How did you learn to not get "suckered" and "falling for those fake-outs"?
Teresa:	Practice, experience, making mistakes, umm . . . learning the sector and the big players, talking to other traders, stuff like that. Another huge part is becoming comfortable with your surroundings, things like the software you use, the resources you go to, the environment you trade in.
Trading Coach:	That's interesting. What do you mean by that?
Teresa:	Well, basically all of those things that you take for granted can end up being huge distractions to you, believe it or not. I never thought so until I changed some of them around and started to feel comfortable with

(continued)

> my system. It was amazing, all of sudden, I was able to focus all of my attention on the market and my trades. I started to see things that I normally missed and stopped wasting my time and energy on irrelevant factors.
>
> **Trading Coach:** And that is what turned things around for you?
>
> **Teresa:** Well, not exclusively, I'm sure, I still had to work at my game plan and gain experience along the way. But one thing is for sure: I may never have reached the level that I am at today if I had never learned how to tune into what I was doing rather than wasting my energy dealing with all of the extra distractions.

Teresa worked hard at learning what it took for her to become a successful online trading athlete. As our conversation with her illustrates, she went through some tough times at first but eventually learned that she could help herself achieve her potential by putting herself in the right environment so she could tune in to what she was doing rather than trying to block out distractions. In contrast to Teresa are traders like Freddy, who have not been able to reach their potential in the trading game because they think that focusing is about learning how to block out the distractions.

FLUSTERED FREDDY

Freddy has been in the trading game for just around six months now but he feels that he is not progressing as quickly as he should. Every time he sits down to trade he does not know what to do first. He has tried several different software packages to find the simplest one but he complains that, "No matter what software I use, there is just too much information for me to go through to be able to make any trading decisions."

Trading Coach:	Hey Freddy, how are things going today?
Freddy:	Same as usual, nothing really going on.
Trading Coach:	What do you mean nothing going on, I saw that the NASDAQ took a pretty serious hit, it was down over 120 points by 1:00 P.M.
Freddy:	Yeah, I know, I guess I meant nothing going on for me.
Trading Coach:	I see . . . well how many trades did you make today?
Freddy:	Two . . . I just couldn't decide on what to do. There are too many things going on at once. All those colors flashing on the screen, all those news releases, all those different stocks to trade. It's overwhelming.
Trading Coach:	Yeah, I know what you mean. It's easy to feel lost and confused in the market.
Freddy *(sighs)*:	I just thought by now, after trading for six months, that it would get easier but it only seems to be more difficult. The longer I watch the market, the more information I find out

(continued)

	about that is available to me, and the more stocks I find that look like they would be good to trade.
Trading Coach:	Have you tried any mental strategies to help you deal with filtering through the huge amounts of information?
Freddy:	Yeah, I guess . . . I read in a book once about how to block things out so you can make good decisions. The book talked about writing down all of the things that distract you from your task and I'll admit, I tried it but there is just too much to block out. My list had more than 50 things on it . . . it ended up stressing me out big time so I gave up.
Trading Coach:	Freddy, I'm sorry to hear that you had that stressful experience. But I think it may have been a good lesson to learn. You see, you are absolutely right, there are way too many things to try to block out. We encourage our clients to tune in to what they are doing and not try to block things out. It really comes down to a matter of focusing your energies on one or two things (tuning in) rather than worrying about a ton of things (blocking out). Does that make any sense?
Freddy:	Actually, it really does. So I see, by . . . what did you call it again?
Trading Coach:	Tuning in.

Freddy:	Oh, yeah, sorry . . . by tuning in, I'll be able to get rid of some of the anxiety that I am feeling and make quicker decision?
Trading Coach:	Possibly, but it really is up to you. You see, tuning in is just a concept that only works if you practice doing it.

As the previous conversation suggests, it is apparent that Freddy's trading difficulties are tied into his inability to filter through the thousands of distractions that occur during the typical trading day. By encouraging Freddy to tune in to what he is doing rather than trying to block out every single distraction, he may eventually be able to take his game to the next level as an online trading athlete.

So what can we learn from Teresa and Freddy? They both are playing the same game but by different rules. Teresa has and will continue to achieve success while Freddy may never be able to reach his potential unless he begins to learn how to tune in rather than block out.

Over time, elite athletes as well as expert online trading athletes learn to focus in on those factors that will give them the edge in competitive situations. The art of concentration is learning to stay focused on these important factors while ignoring things that are irrelevant. In basketball, for example, if a player only blocked out distractions (crowd noise, other players, fatigue, and so on), he or she would not know where the out of bounds lines were much less which of his or her teammates were open. Instead, the basketball player learns to filter through the confusion of the game and focus in on the essentials of the current skill being performed (the dribble, a pass, a shot, playing defense, and so on). Just like elite athletes, online trading athletes can learn from experience, and by tapping into their natural learning style, they can filter through distractions (rather than blocking them out) and begin tuning in on the essentials of their current trading position.

Sport psychologists call the important aspects of performance on which athletes learn to focus performance cues. For an elite tennis player, for example, important performance cues to pay attention to are the upper body position of your opponent just before a serve. The challenge for an online trading athlete is to determine which are the important performance cues in the online trading environment (trends, momentum, relative strength, order flow in the market, big players entering or leaving, and so on).

USE PERFORMANCE CUES

When we focus on the right things during trading, we increase our chances of success. But when we get sidetracked into thinking about things that are irrelevant, or worse, counterproductive, we increase our chances of failure. Top athletes learn that during the heat of competition, it helps to focus on one or two simple things that remind them what to do in order to succeed. Sport psychologists call these simple reminders performance cues.

Skier Tommy Moe used a performance cue with great effectiveness at the 1994 Winter Olympic Games in Lillehammer. Tommy was the surprise winner of the men's downhill alpine competition. Although he had never won a World Cup event in his career, Tommy blasted down the Olympic course on Kvitfjell faster than any other competitor, winning the first gold medal of the games for the United States. After the race, he was asked to comment on his strategy. Moe replied, "I just kept my thoughts real simple. I wanted to focus on making my turns with a strong edge on the outside ski, and keeping my hands forward. I knew if I concentrated on those two things, I would ski fast. That's all I wanted to do."

By winning the Olympic gold medal, Tommy Moe laid claim to the title of the fastest man on skis in the world. Yet his performance cues on race day were surprisingly simple. Even rank novices are advised to make their turns by edging the outside ski and to keep their hands pointing down the hill. But by keeping his focus simple, Tommy was able to place all his attention on the job of going fast. He did not try to block out all the many distractions of an Olympic competition—the huge crowds, the global television audience, the good race times of his competitors, or even his place in the starting order. Instead, he tuned into his body and its interaction with the skis and the snow, feeling the rhythm of a great run—the feeling between his body and the snow that allowed him to choose the winning line on every turn.

How do you go about choosing the important factors that will help you become the very best online trading athlete you can be?

SELECTING A PERFORMANCE CUE

In all pressure situations, there are thousands of possible thoughts for you to concentrate on, but only a few will help you get the job done successfully. How do you choose your performance cue?

Here are three simple guidelines to help you. We have found these basic sport psychology principles to be effective guides for both athletes and for our trading clients.

GUIDELINE #1: KEEP YOUR PERFORMANCE CUES SIMPLE

It is helpful to tune in to some simple ideas to guide you through even complicated situations. You can confuse yourself with thoughts that are long and complicated. Many clients of ours have told us of trading disasters caused by "paralysis by analysis," the problem of thinking too much during a transaction. Top athletes often talk about "playing brain dead" or "not thinking about anything at all" when they are trying to perform at their best. As Mets fans, we remember third baseman Ray Knight being interviewed after he had made a key hit in the New York Mets improbable three-run rally in the bottom of the 10th inning of Game 6 of the 1986 World Series. The interviewer asked him, "Ray, what were you thinking about in that critical at-bat?" Ray responded, "Nothing! I wasn't thinking about anything!" Sport psychologists call this automatic behavior, and indeed, when you are really concentrating at a high level it feels like you are performing on automatic pilot.

Teach yourself to focus on the basics first. The more skilled you are and the more experience you have, the more important it is to begin with the basics and allow your expertise to guide you almost unconsciously. Remember gold medal winner Tommy Moe? He chose two of the most basic thoughts any skier can have to guide his gold medal run down the mountain.

To help you develop your own simple performance cues, we have included a list of some of the performance cues we have heard from top-level traders over the years.

- See the trade, push the button
- Jump in and stay flexible
- Buy it low, sell it high (or sell it high, buy it low)
- Know your out before you get in

- Just hit singles
- Open it, close it
- Extend your profit, cut your losses

GUIDELINE #2: MAKE YOUR PERFORMANCE CUES POSITIVE

It is a simple idea to avoid negative thinking when you are trying to concentrate. Yet time and time again we see athletes and traders in high-pressure situations who fall into the trap of setting themselves up for failure. They do this by worrying about mistakes they have made or trying to avoid making a mistake in the future.

When we think of something bad and it ends up coming true, we call it a self-fulfilling prophecy. Why does this happen? To illustrate this, we will tell you about one of our clients who we will call Jo Ann. Jo Ann was an experienced trader who had achieved success for the past three years as a momentum trader. Recently she found that her profits had been declining and that she was taking on significantly larger losers than she ever had before. She tried everything: decreasing the size of her position, reading books on new chart reading techniques, trading at different times of the day, but none of these worked consistently for her. After talking with her, she admitted that sometimes when she is in a trade, she hears this little voice in her head that yells out, "Don't let this turn into a big loser again."

No matter how hard she tried she said, "I just can't get that annoying little voice out of my head. Actually, what I have found is that the harder I try to get rid of it, the louder it becomes and the more distracted I am." While Jo Ann struggles with this inner voice, she begins to second-guess herself and either gets out too soon or rides it out too long after the market has turned, resulting in a big loser, thereby, completing her self-fulfilling prophecy.

(Before we move on, we should point out two things. Jo Ann was not schizophrenic and she was not suffering from a split personality disorder.)

Jo Ann was simply going through what almost all elite competitors experience every now and then—negative thinking. In order to help Jo Ann, we had to explain to her that her negative thinking pattern was causing her to question herself. Of course, the age-old question remains, which came first? Did her negative thinking cause poor performance or did her poor performance cause negative thinking? The truth is that both were feeding each other, so in order to stop the pattern, Jo Ann had to learn to use a new positive performance cue that would help her tune in to success rather than trying to block out failure. This seemed to make sense to her and she chose to change her performance cue to "Focus on the trade and ride it like a wave." After a few days of working together on controlling and changing that "annoying little voice in her head," Jo Ann was able to get herself back on track by creating a positive performance cue that allowed her to tune in to her trading position rather than try to block everything else out.

GUIDELINE #3: FOCUS ON YOUR STRENGTHS

Years of experience have shown us that elite athletes know that the time to worry about weakness is during practice and that it is not until a day or two before the competition that they begin to focus on their strengths. As a result, once the game begins, they are prepared to put it all on the line so they can achieve their potential.

In contrast, the poorer performers did just the opposite. During practice they tend to think about their strengths and how good they are and then just before competition, or even during the competition itself, they start thinking about their weaknesses.

As an online trading athlete, you can learn from the successful elite athletes by using your practice time to analyze your weakness and work on them, and then, just prior to the opening bell, remind yourself of your strengths.

The following is a list of things that you can say to yourself to help remind you to focus on your strengths before you begin to trade.

- I may not be the quickest trader in the world, but I have control and desire and that will make me successful.
- I have practiced my relaxation strategies and am ready to use them if I have trouble staying focused.
- I have had success competing in the past and this is no different so I will be successful again.
- I have an incredible work ethic, which has helped me to achieve my goals when I put my mind to it.
- I am aware of my limitations and when to get out of a bad trade.
- I do a great job at setting goals, sticking to them, and reaching them.
- I have trained myself to stay disciplined so now it is time to put it into action.
- I am very familiar with the software and if the unexpected happens, I know how to handle it.
- I always remain calm, especially when things start to get crazy.
- I have organized my screen so I know how to get the information I need at a moments notice.

YOUR PERFORMANCE CUES

There is a reason that successful athletes at all levels and in all sports use performance cues to stay at the top of their game and maintain concentration—it is because it works! In most cases, performance cues simply act as a reminder to the athletes but once they practice using them, these cues become an automatic trigger, which enables the athletes to refocus, maintain concentration, and win. Keep in mind that a performance cue should be personalized and specific to the individual. Ideally, as an online trading athlete, you want to create performance cues that are "catchy" so they are easy to remember and fun to use. The following are some sport specific examples of performance cues that we have heard over the years:

Golf

- "Finish the turn"
- "Smooth and solid"

Baseball/Softball

- "Drop and drive"
- "Load and explode"

Tennis

- "Stick and mash"
- "Toss and cross"

Volleyball

- "Set and spike"
- "Bump and bury"

Football

- "Snap and spiral"
- "Turn and burn"

Focusing on these words initially allows an athlete to remove all distractions from his or her mind and focus on the current task. Just as you stop thinking about the hairy gorilla when you think of a pink elephant, a golfer who is focusing on a "smooth and solid" swing has no time to think of distracting thoughts such as, "I wish those guys would stop talking" or "I hope I don't land in the drink." Once the action is initiated, the athlete's automatic pilot takes over, and the athlete begins to really enjoy the moment and to focus totally on the here-and-now. We will discuss this aspect of high-level performance in detail in the next chapter.

For the online trading athlete, a performance cue needs to be different from what you are normally saying to yourself while you are in your trading stadium looking at price histories, volume, news releases, and so on. Here are some performance cues we have found that online trading athletes successfully use:

- "Find it and ride it"
- "Patient and profit"
- "Be 3-D: desire, discipline, dedication"

Now it is your turn. What are some essential, simple, positive performance cues that you can use to focus your attention and help you maintain concentration?

My Performance Cues

_____

_____

Go ahead and keep modifying and adding to this list over time. You might pick up tips from other traders, the web, or magazines and books. Have fun with it! Remember that it is not the words themselves that are the critical ingredient for good concentration. It is your ability to tune in on the essentials rather than having to spend energy blocking out distractions. We have heard from golfers who have been given a new swing tip by their instructor and have gone out and played a great round that all of a sudden, they believe they have discovered the secret of the golf swing! Yet two weeks later, they are playing their usual left-and-right, inconsistent golf again. Why does their belief in their new swing unlock their potential for a round or two and then seemingly fade away? The answer lies in the secret of tuning in. For the first round or so, the new swing thought is just that—new. The golfer pays attention to it and finds it fresh and inspiring. They get into a rhythm and start trusting their swing. It works!

But a round or two later, it is no longer fresh. They try to focus on the swing thought but their mind wanders. They start to get too technical again, worrying about the size of their hip turn, the angle of their swing plane, and the positioning of their feet. They start to look up and see the hazards in front of them, the out-of-bounds down the right-hand side of the fairway. They are no longer tuning in, they are struggling to block out. It was not their new swing thought that suddenly lost its effectiveness, it was the golfer who stopped concentrating fully.

Let us look at some examples from a typical trading day. Each of the following situations is a common one that you might experience on any given day. If you are paying attention to that situation, are you tuning in or blocking out? We have given you the answers to the first two situations. See how well you do in identifying the remainder of them. After each situation respond with whether it is an example of blocking out or tuning in.

- You found out that earnings came out yesterday — *Blocking Out*
- The earnings report was in five minutes so you flattened your position — *Tuning In*
- CNBC issued a special report and you did not see it — _____
- Telecom sector is tanking and you look at other sectors for opportunities — _____
- The trader next to you is on fire and you do not know what he is trading — _____
- Whisper number = $.10, actual = $.14, that is down $.05 from last quarter — _____
- You traded all day without taking any breaks — _____
- Bonds are up, Dow is down, S&Ps are steady, BioTech is hot, Chip Makers are down — _____

Now that you clearly see the difference between blocking out and tuning in, keep in mind that to boost your powers of concentration, you must practice. How do you do that? In the final section of this chapter we show you how.

PRACTICE, PRACTICE, PRACTICE

Question: How much time do you think a successful golfer spends practicing the short game?
Answer: At least half, if not more, of their practice time.

Question: How many hours do you think a hitter spends in the batting cage?

Answer: Hundreds.

Question: How many serves do you think a tennis player practices?

Answer: Thousands.

As an online trading athlete, you are no different. To achieve success, you need to practice. Just as elite athletes practice their physical skills, online trading athletes should practice their mental skills.

Having said this, in order for you to see some results, you need to put in some quality time and practice concentrating and then relaxing for short periods. Keep in mind that the adult human brain can only concentrate for 7 to 15 minutes at a time and then it is daydream time!

What this means is that in order to maintain quality concentration, you need to be able to turn it on and off. This is where the performance cue comes in again. The cue helps you turn it on and then after a period of time you turn it off. We know it sounds unusual but with a little practice you will see results and be able to improve both the level and duration of your concentration skills.

Now what happens if you forget to turn it off? Well, the light bulb eventually burns out. You begin to daydream and lose concentration. Consider this example. How many times do you miss a five-foot putt and end up six feet from the cup (on the other side of the hole). You then spend the next minute or two trying to line up your next putt while reliving your first missed putt. As you approach your second putt, you are still thinking about the first bad putt and then—yes, you guessed it—you end up leaving it short. Forget about par—on in three, out in six. Does this sound familiar?

Aside from snowballing one bad shot into two or three or four more, what you forgot to do was turn the cue off after the first putt and then turn the cue on as you approached the second putt. Misreads and physical errors are part of the game, no matter what level you are at. What we want you to realize is that same thing applies to online trading athletes. If you make one poor trade, fine. Acknowledge it, and then move on. If you are not willing to move on, then do yourself a favor and pick up your ball and walk off the hole. You will find that it will be a lot cheaper in the long run than if you spent the whole day counting and reliving your bad trades.

When top athletes or successful traders lose their concentration, the cause is always one of three things: ruminating about mistakes made in the past; worrying about what will happen in the future, or being unhappy with the present situation. In all three cases, the cause of the loss of concentration is not the past or future event itself. It is the way we react to that event. In the next chapter we learn how to achieve our true potential by remaining in the here-and-now and playing this game one trade at a time.

---◆---

Concentration: Tuning In to Success

- Tuning in instead of blocking out

- Using performance cues

- Selecting a performance cue
    — Guideline #1: Keep your performance cues simple
    — Guideline #2: Make your performance cues positive
    — Guideline #3: Focus on your strengths

- Practice, practice, practice

CHAPTER NINE

ENJOYING THE MOMENT: PLAYING THE GAME ONE TRADE AT A TIME

Take a look at the following scenarios and see if you can identify what they have in common. What mistake are these athletes making that is preventing them from playing to their potential?

- A batter strikes out his first at-bat and he is still fuming over it in the next half-inning when he is in the field. He ends up making a fielding error on a routine groundball because he is still thinking about the strikeout he made.

- A tennis player wins the first set, 6–0, blowing out her opponent. After racing to a 3–0 lead in the second set, she begins to wonder who she will play in the next round. She remembers it could be a high-seeded player who is always a challenge. But before she knows it, she has lost the second set, 4–6, and is fighting tooth-and-nail to survive the match.

- A batter hits a homerun in his first at-bat and then coasts on that at-bat for the rest of the game. He feels so good about his homerun that he loses focus during his subsequent at-bats and does not reach base again. His team loses, 5–4.

- The field goal kicker misses a 35-yard field goal to end the half. In the fourth quarter his team is down by two with three seconds on the clock and he gets the call to attempt another 35-yard field goal. This time, however, the game is on the line. He steps up to the ball determined to overcome his first mistake. This time he will show them that he is a good kicker! Oops—wide right again!

- A soccer team scores four unanswered goals in the first half. Despite their coach's pep talk at halftime they play the second half with less intensity, a shadow of the team they were in the first half. They lose their momentum while the other team gains theirs, scoring four goals to tie the game.

What does each situation have in common? We know, because we have all been guilty of similar mistakes. Each of these athletes or teams was either hanging on to the past or worrying about the future. As a result, they did not focus 100 percent on the present. In any competitive situation, the smallest detail can make the difference between winning and losing, so wasting energy in this way almost guarantees less than stellar performance. Only by staying in the here-and-now can we always give our truly best effort on a task.

The same holds true for the online trading athlete. Here are some common examples of online trading athletes not staying in the here-and-now.

- In the middle of a busy day, a trader begins to dream about profits before they are realized. He might even be thinking so far ahead that he starts to imagine what he will buy with those profits.

- After a bad day, a trader goes home and three hours later he is still analyzing the mistakes he made earlier in the day. The market is no longer open, there is nothing he can do, but in his mind he is imagining how things might be different if he had not made those trades.
- While initiating a new transaction, an online trading athlete is still sick to her stomach over a bad trade made earlier in the day. She cannot get it out of her head.
- After a great trade, an online trading athlete is still thinking about how much better it would have been if he had only taken a larger position or held the position a little longer or . . . the list goes on.

No matter how you look at it, a trader who is focused on something other than the current trade is giving up the mental edge that he or she could have in the trading game. This edge is so hard to earn and so hard to keep, that it is a shame if an online trading athlete tosses it away by not understanding the power of staying focused. In this chapter we show you how important it is to hold to that axiom of "one trade at a time," and provide you with strategies for living life in the present, not in the past or future. If put into practice, these strategies will help you enjoy your trading activities on a regular basis.

THE BASIC PRINCIPLES OF HAPPINESS

University of Chicago psychologist, Mihaly Csikszentmihalyi, provided the most elegant explanation we have seen of what it means to enjoy life. Csikszentmihalyi has dedicated his life's work to understanding the psychology of happiness, and in the process found that it is not a particular activity that makes people happy, but a particular approach to an activity.

Csikszentmihalyi and colleagues found that people were not necessarily happier when they were relaxing or taking time off. In fact, quite the opposite was true. Many people were happiest in the middle of an engaging project at work. What seemed to make people truly happy was any activity that was challenging, interesting, and enjoyable. Thus, people were most happy in diverse activities such as work, playing chess, mountain climbing, playing a musical instrument, running, and, of course, having sex. By studying the commonality of experiences that make people happy, Csikszentmihalyi discovered that it was how people approached an activity that made all the difference. When asked to describe what it felt like to be engaged in an enjoyable activity, respondents from all over the world used very similar descriptions. They also used very similar terms to convey the reasons why they enjoyed the activity. After years of research, Csikszentmihalyi was able to identify eight elements that are common to most experiences that make people truly happy.

We believe that if athletes and online trading athletes can apply these basic principles to their work, they will be not only happy, but also successful. These principles help define what it means to choose a here-and-now focus. In fact, Csikszentmihalyi calls the experience of true happiness being in the "flow," and what athlete does not want to be in the flow? Let us look at each of the eight elements of happiness, and examine how it applies to the world of the online trading athlete.

1. A CHALLENGING TASK AT WHICH WE MAY SUCCEED

Enjoyment in any activity comes when the challenge of the activity is equal to the skill of the participant. If the task is too easy, success does not mean much and we are more likely to experience boredom than pleasure. If the task is too difficult, success seems unlikely and we are more likely to experience anxiety. This is what makes sports exciting at so many levels. An example would be as follows: "I do not have the skills of Pete Sampras, but I can enjoy a good hard match at my club on a Saturday morning. The challenge is just right for my skill level, and I have a good chance of experiencing success."

The online trading athlete will experience the greatest satisfaction when they are challenged but not overwhelmed by their work. A rookie trader venturing into the sink-or-swim online trading game may experience nothing but terror. However, faced with trading choices that he is prepared for and knowledgeable about, he can eventually experience the joys of well-executed trades.

2. THE MERGING OF ACTION AND AWARENESS

This factor is best illustrated by the athlete who is so in tune with their game that they lose track of everything else except what they are doing. They are in perfect synchrony with their body. Perhaps you have experienced something like this while out on a long run. You are so totally focused on your pace and rhythm that you forget about the pain and the heat; you feel only your heartbeat and your legs and arms moving in harmony.

A trader who is operating at the highest level describes a similar experience. They are not thinking of anything else but the trades and the market, and they almost lose touch with the world around them because they are so engrossed in their activity.

3. THE TASK HAS CLEAR GOALS

Those engaged in their favorite activity usually have a clear sense of where they are headed. The chess player trying to win a game, the golfer trying to shoot a low score, the artist creating a sculpture—all have an idea of what is required for them to be successful.

This principle applies to the world of the online trading athlete who faces clear goals and choices throughout the day: make money, by buying at the right time, in the appropriate amount, and selling after the right interval. The rules of the game are almost too simple, but some of the most enjoyable activities available to us have such simple boundaries.

4. THE TASK PROVIDES IMMEDIATE FEEDBACK

This element of happiness is closely tied to the one before because the pursuit of one's goals usually provides feedback about one's progress. The chess player sees the opportunity for an exciting gambit developing, the golfer is buoyed by making successive birdies, the sculptor knows in his heart that the piece looks right.

The online trading athlete has almost too much feedback available to him or her. Stock quotes, computer technology, and Internet access have combined to provide the trader with a multitude of options for assessing the success or failure of a transaction. The traders who seem to prosper most are those who can sort through the mass of information available to them and see the underlying trends.

5. TOTAL CONCENTRATION ON THE TASK AT HAND

Another common characteristic of the flow experience is that while engaged in the activity, all other worries and concerns seem to fade into the background. The athlete is totally locked into the game and is not even aware of the 90,000 people in the stands cheering. Csikszentmihalyi shares the words of the great American hurdler, Edwin Moses, who said this about his level of concentration while competing: "Your mind has to be absolutely clear. The fact that you have to cope with your opponent, jet lag, different foods, sleeping in hotels, and personal problems has to be erased from consciousness—as if they didn't exist." (*Flow: The Pscyhology of Optimal Experience* [New York: Harper & Row, 1990], 59).

As we discussed in the previous chapter, the art of effective concentration distinguishes the successful online trading athlete from the mediocre. The trader who is truly focused is tuned in to what he needs to do and does not waste energy worrying about factors he cannot control.

6. A FEELING OF CONTROL OVER YOUR ACTIONS

If you have ever watched a child learning a new skill such as riding a bike, you know what Csikszentmihalyi is talking about here. First come a series of failures, then gradually new skills are gained, until the child can ride without falling; often they yell and whoop in happiness. Any difficult activity provides this same feeling. At some point you have mastered it enough so that you can actually do it well—and the feeling is fantastic. Most golfers remember the course where they were playing and the hole they were on when they sank their first birdie or eagle, and the rush of adrenaline and joy that accompanied marking down that score.

Online trading athletes also know the feeling that comes with their first winning trade, their first big winner, their first good month, or their mastery of a new sector, a new technology, or a new approach. There is a paradox here, which Csikszentmihalyi points out, in that the trader has no real control over the outcome of their trades, but they do have control over the quality of their trades. It is this feeling of control, of doing their job well, that is most satisfying to the successful trader.

7. A Loss of Self-Consciousness

This element of happiness is the loss of awareness of self-scrutiny. During many, perhaps most, activities we are usually aware of the thought in our minds, "How am I doing?" This thought causes self-scrutiny, and if we do not measure up, can cause anxiety and concern. When you are in the flow, these self-analytical thoughts disappear, at least for the moment. You are aware only of what you are doing and how you feel doing it. You do not care what others think of you. For example, a figure skater stops worrying about the judges and her parents and whether she is meeting their expectations; she is aware only of the music and her movements.

The trader who is worrying about how he or she is doing is wasting precious energy that could be devoted to focusing on the transaction. When in the flow, the online trading athlete stops asking the questions "Is this trade going well?" and instead waits for the right moments to open and close positions.

8. The Transformation of Time

This last characteristic may not be the most common element of the experience of happiness, but it is one of the most interesting. When it does occur, which is not frequently, it is described as either a sense of time slowing down, or a sense that time has flown by. We have heard athletes describe both sensations to us. A tennis player tells us that when he is in the flow, time seems to slow down and he has much longer than usual to decide on which shot to hit and where to place it. A football player who just played a terrific game told us that he only remembers the kickoff and the high-fives at the game's end—nothing in between. Both descriptions indicate that something special happened, perhaps as result of the intense concentration that goes along with the flow experience.

Many traders have had similar experiences. Often it is the feeling on a good day of, "Where did the day go?" It seems that the opening bells rings, there is a brief pause for lunch, and then the closing bell sounds. This is usually a sign that the trader has been so engrossed in their trading that they did not have time to watch the clock. In contrast, when the day is going badly, time seems to move in slow motion, every minute another painful taste of reality. Either way, time has an odd way of transforming depending on our perception of our situation.

To illustrate this, we are going to tell you about a momentum-trading client of ours, who we will call Susie. Susie had been trading out of her house for over a year when she first contacted our firm. She was a full-time mom and now that her two kids were growing up, she found that she had more free time so she decided to do something for herself and began to explore the world of online trading.

IN THE TRADING FLOW

Susie: I never really thought it would turn into a full-time job. I really was just trying to find something new and fun to do while my husband was at work.

(continued)

Trading Coach:	And did you find that something in trading?
Susie:	Well, at first, no. I would be so nervous when I made a trade. My hands would shake, and I could not sit still. I would worry about what would happen if the stock went down after I bought it or even how to know when to sell it if it went up. It was really confusing for some time.
Trading Coach:	Sounds like you had a pretty normal introduction to the trading experience.
Susie:	I guess so. Funny thing is though, I would get so caught up in the moment.
Trading Coach:	Really? And what "moment" would that be?
Susie:	I guess the moment of making trades and watching the market move. I would sit there for what seemed like 10 or 15 minutes and I would look up and it would be 1:30 P.M. already. My whole day just disappeared. It really was quite amazing how that happened.
Trading Coach:	So was that ok with you that your whole day seemed to "disappear"?
Susie:	At first, no, because I had only wanted to do this trading thing part-time, you see. Now it was turning into a full-time job.
Trading Coach:	And did that bother you?

Susie:	Actually, not really. I kind of enjoyed it. I felt energized. My days were exciting and I was finally doing something for myself after years of being an at-home mom. Don't get me wrong, I loved being an at-home mom but now that I have been trading, I don't think I could go back to what I was doing before.
Trading Coach:	We hear that from a lot of new traders. So tell us, how is it different when you make money versus losing money?
Susie:	What do you mean? Making money is a whole lot more fun!
Trading Coach: *(laughing)*	You are right, sorry, that was a bad question. What I meant was the time factor. How is that different? Does the day go quicker or slower when you are making or losing money?
Susie:	Definitely faster when I am making money. Time just seems to fly by. It's like I don't want it to end. When I am making good money and things are going my way, I actually get mad when the market closes. I can't wait for the next day.
Trading Coach:	What about those days when you are losing money?
Susie:	It's a totally different experience. Somehow the day seems longer. I

(continued)

> | | can't exactly explain it but it just seems to drag. You know what I mean? |
> |---|---|
> | **Trading Coach:** | I sure do. |
> | **Susie:** | I don't know, maybe its because I begin to become frustrated and more aware of all of the distractions around me. Whatever it is, it's the pits. I'm just glad I have had more quick days than slow ones. |

As Susie's story illustrates, time does seem to have a way of transforming, which is usually connected to whether the trader is having a good day or bad day in the market.

WHAT HAPPENS WHEN YOU ENJOY THE MOMENT?

The aspect of Csikszentmihalyi's research that we find most fascinating is the suggestion, heard over and over again from top performers in all fields, that they perform their best when they are truly enjoying their performance—when they are in the flow. Clearly, in order to get into the flow, you must stay focused on the task at hand, fully concentrating on the challenge, and putting all of your energy into doing the task as well as possible.

This corresponds precisely with our experience. The successful online trading athletes we have spoken to make a habit out of staying in the here-and-now, rather than thinking about what was or what could be. The bottom line is they work long and hard at becoming experts at playing the game one pitch at a time and trading—one trade at a time.

Yet, entire books have been written about the challenge of staying focused, so we know it is not an easy thing to do. What are the major distractions to staying focused in the here-and-now, and what can you do about them?

STAYING ANGRY WITH YOURSELF AFTER A MISTAKE

One of the greatest threats to being in the flow is regret: "I should never have made that mistake," or "It would have turned out differently if I had done something else." The energy we spend replaying mistakes in our mind and fantasizing over how much better things would be right now if we had not made that mistake is completely wasted. One thing is certain: until time travel is invented, there is no way to correct the mistakes of the past.

Here is the story of a former client of ours, who we will call Dave, who made a habit out of beating himself up after a bad trade. Dave is in his early 30s and had been an All-American wrestler in college. As a result of his years of wrestling at the elite level, he was probably one of the most disciplined and hardworking people we have ever met. Dave is all about business. He has a touch of obsessiveness in his personality and accepted nothing but perfection from his performance, regardless of what he was doing. Dave's greatest strengths in wrestling translated to both his greatest strengths and weaknesses in the online trading game. He has spent hours working on his trading style and has conditioned himself to become what he believes to be the "picture perfect textbook trader." Along the way, Dave has been in touch with our firm, occasionally contacting us for what he called "maintenance." Despite the brief time we spent working with Dave, we have a solid grasp of what type of personality we are dealing with because of our vast previous experience providing athletic performance consulting to elite wrestlers.

One Friday afternoon, Dave contacted our firm for one of his maintenance checks and he began to grumble about a trade he had made.

Dave:	I still do not understand why I sold that stock short.
Trading Coach:	What trade are you talking about?
Dave:	Those 1,500 shares I shorted last Monday.
Trading Coach:	What company?
Dave:	AMGN.
Trading Coach:	Oh, where are you short from?
Dave:	I'm not anymore, I closed the position out on Tuesday. I just can't believe that I was that stupid!
Trading Coach:	How did you trade the rest of this week?
Dave:	Trade? What for? I need to get my act together first so I don't make a stupid mistake like that again. What I did is totally unacceptable. Never mind, I am just going to deal with this myself.

At this point in time, it became clear that Dave's perfectionist mentality was preventing him from moving past the poor trade he had made earlier in the week and from seeking further help on the matter. What we want to point out through Dave's story is that he was unable to function for the entire week because he was still caught up in reliving his poor trade from Monday. Although Dave's case is an extreme example (primarily fueled by his unique personality), most online trading athletes get tangled up in staying angry with themselves after they make a mistake. To be successful at the online trading game, you need to be able to roll with the bad and focus on the good and move on to the next trade.

WORRYING ABOUT THE FUTURE

Another very common threat to being in the flow is worrying about what might happen. Many online trading athletes are particularly susceptible to this distraction. "What if the Fed doesn't cut rates as they are expected?" "I might be in big trouble if I take this position and things don't work out." "What's going on with that trade I made this morning? I hope it goes well. I can't afford to be wrong." All the energy spent worrying about these things is also wasted because none of them may ever come to pass. We are not fortune-tellers (If you are, why on earth are you reading this book? Go out and make money!). The saying "Don't save your best for later because there may not be a later" was written with this exact scenario in mind. The high-performing online trading athlete expends energy thinking about the problem immediately before them and does not waste energy worrying about problems that may never occur.

UNHAPPINESS WITH THE PRESENT

Another threat to a state of flow is fretting over dissatisfaction with the way things are. For online trading athletes, this can take the form of worrying that you are not getting reliable information, watching a news report on CNBC with alarm, being jealous of another trader who is on a hot streak, worrying that you do not have enough analytical tools to make good decisions, wanting to read some more reports before jumping into the market, and so on, and so on. Just about anything can distract us from the task at hand if we let it. Take Adam, a client of ours who has a habit of trusting no one.

Adam sent an e-mail to our firm wanting to know more about what we do and if we could help him. We responded to his e-mail telling him about what we did and that the answer to his second question depended on what he thought he needed help with. Several weeks later we received a second e-mail from Adam indicating that he thought that we could help and he wanted to set up an appointment.

Adam was a position trader who had been trading out of his house for a year and half. He admitted that he had not "been as successful as he should be," but that it was not entirely his fault.

| **Trading Coach:** | So tell me what it is that has been preventing you from being "as successful as you should be. |
| **Adam:** | It's real simple. I have been through 15 different trading analysis software packages and all of them |

are inadequate. In addition, in the last six months I have transferred my brokerage account to five different firms because none of them can provide me with quality service.

Trading Coach: That's got to be pretty stressful and annoying.

Adam: You don't know the half of it!

Trading Coach: Hmm, tell me some more about the analysis software package issue. You said they were "inadequate." Would you mind explaining what you mean?

Adam: Come on, have you ever used any of them?

Trading Coach: Actually, I have and I agree with you, some of them are pretty awkward but there are some good ones out there too.

Adam: Well, I don't know which ones you have used but the ones I have tried are all put together backwards. They make no sense.

Trading Coach: I can understand how you feel. Have you asked other traders which ones they use?

Adam: Yeah, but they'll never tell me if they have a good one. Why would they? I mean, if they tell me their secrets and I start making money, then that means there's less money out there for them.

(continued)

By the way, this is an extremely common misconception. There is plenty of profit out there to go around and as we pointed out earlier in this book, the only person you are in competition with in the trading game is yourself!

Trading Coach:	That's an interesting way to view the market.
Adam:	What, you don't agree with that?
Trading Coach:	No, not really but we can talk about that more later. Let's get back to the issue of software packages.
Adam:	Fine.
Trading Coach:	Have you ever tried to trade without using one?
Adam:	No, not really.
Trading Coach:	You may want to try that out. You see software packages are great ways to enhance your analysis skills but if you are becoming annoyed with their design, then they may become a distraction to you and actually limit your performance potential.
Adam:	I guess that kinda makes sense.
Trading Coach:	Good, now let's talk about how you have transferred your account to five different firms.
Adam:	Oh, that's a whole other issue.
Trading Coach:	Really? I seem to think that there may be some similarities between the two.
Adam:	Oh yeah? How so?
Trading Coach:	Well, for one, you are dissatisfied with both of them.

Adam:	Yeah.
Trading Coach:	And second, because you are focused on them, they both seem to be distracting you from reaching your potential as a trader.
(Long pause)	
Adam:	That does seem to make sense!

Adam is extremely and consistently unhappy with the present. As a result, he is consumed and distracted by external factors. His level of distraction has prevented him from focusing on the market and he is constantly feeling that he is being misinformed. This overwhelming feeling of misinformation that he regularly experiences may simply be because he is not able to keep himself up to date on current events because he is too busy switching and learning software packages and/or switching brokerage accounts. Adam's chosen trading style (position trader) relies heavily on chart analysis, overall market performance, and economic indicators. For this reason, it is no mystery why he has not been a successful trader in the past: it is most likely a result of his unhappiness with the present.

There are really only two options we face when we are distracted. We can try to change the distraction, which is the path most people take, or we can choose to tune in to what is important, and leave the distraction behind (see Chapter 8). The distraction has no power over us if we do not pay attention to it.

All the concentration techniques we discussed in the previous chapter can be used successfully to overcome the three challenges. It is with the power of our own mind that we: (1) let the past go, (2) leave the future out there for us to find, and (3) choose to leave the distraction unattended.

It takes some energy and concentration to do these, but the rewards are well worth it. The experience of flow is waiting for us if we can free up our energy to truly enjoy the moment at hand, and to revel in the challenge that we are faced with in the here-and-now. Before ending this chapter, we conclude with some more practical suggestions for dealing with distractions and staying in the flow.

PLAYING ONE TRADE AT A TIME

We cannot stress it enough—play the game one trade at a time! We know, it is easy to say but hard to do, and believe us it takes hard work and hours of practice.

An interesting thing about competition is that one mistake has a funny way of snowballing into two, three, or more. The key to overcoming the tendency we have to self-destruct is to identify the destructive snowball and break its momentum. You can do this by using your self-talk strategies or even calling a time-out (see Chapter 5). Remember, you need to stay in control of yourself—you do not have any control over the market. If things are moving too fast, then slow down. Take a minute to go back over your game plan and review your mission statement (see Chapter 1). Breathe, recover, refocus, and get back in the game.

Staying in the here-and-now means living in the present moment. Make *this* trade the highest quality one you can. And then when this one is over, make the next decision the quality decision that you have trained for. When you are at bat, focus on the pitcher. When you are in the field, focus on the hitter. Always keep in mind that if you want to become a successful online trading athlete, you have to play this game one trade at a time.

Again, the key is to stay disciplined. If you find that you approach your second shot (trade) still thinking about the first shot (trade), then call a personal time-out and step away for a moment or two and refocus and reenergize to get your concentration back (see Chapter 8).

Ok, great, sounds like a good game plan but how do you put it into action? Here is a simple four-step strategy you can use to recover from distractions that threaten to jolt you out of a here-and-now focus:

1. Identify when you leave the here-and-now
2. Step away and take some time to express your frustrations
3. Write down at least one thing you learned from the mistake
4. Take a deep cleansing breath and get back in the game

Let us walk you through this process by using a golf example of snowballing one bad shot (trade) into two, three, or four bad shots (trades).

IDENTIFY

Ideally, you want to be able to identify when you are out of the here-and-now immediately after the first bad shot, but it may take you two or three or four bad shots (trades) in a row before you wake up. Either way, work at it and realize that the first step is to identify the snowball.

EXPRESS

The second step is to understand that you made the mistake and take some time to acknowledge it. Ok, now comes the fun part. Go ahead, express it. Get it out of you. Yell, curse, throw (try not to break anything important)—do whatever works for you.

What you want to be able to do is symbolically or physically throw that last bad shot (trade) away. For example, a pitcher may throw the rosin bag behind the mound into the ground; a golfer may take off his glove and put it in his pocket; a basketball player may use a towel to wipe the sweat off his face and then throw it on the bench; a trader may write down what the trade was and then throw that piece of paper away, and so on. This is called externalizing your anger and it will help you move past it. Think of it this way, you made the bad shot, so take the time to confront it so that you will be ready to move on. If you do not deal with it now, it is likely to keep gnawing away at you, and worrying about a mistake you have made is a sure way to get out of a here-and-now focus. Ok, are you done yet? No, not yet? Fine, take some more time. Are you done now? Good.

LEARN

Now comes the third step: did you learn from the mistake? That is right, learn. Take a minute to really think about it and write at least one thing down that you can take away from this experience that is going to make you a better trader. That is right, put it on paper so that it will be there for you to look at in the future. You do not need to spend any more time on it. Now, it is time to get your head back in the game.

BREATHE

Now that you have methodically worked through this emotional experience, the fourth step is to simply take a deep, cleansing breath and pick up your club so you can get back on the fairway. (By the way, nice recovery after your first two bad shots! We will put you down for a five. A bogey was not so bad, was it? It is a lot better than that triple that you usually get in those situations!)

THE 10-MINUTE PROMISE

One of the blocks that prevent many online trading athletes from getting into the flow is simply getting started. They hesitate, do more research, answer e-mails, make phone calls, organize their desk—anything but trading. If you are not engaged in the activity of your choice, there is absolutely no chance that you will excel at it, or get in the flow. Often the excuse of the trader is that they "don't feel ready to start" trading.

The trouble with this attitude is that you are letting your feelings dictate your chances of success. The great early American psychologist William James once said, "We are more likely to act ourselves into feeling, than we are to feel ourselves into acting." A wise man! His point is that very often, once we have begun a task, we start to enjoy it. The trick is to start.

A saying that we commonly use is Murphy's Law of Inertia and it applies in these situations. Simply put, Murphy's Law of Inertia states that the longer you wait to start, the less (not more) likely you will be to begin. Over time, inertia gathers its own force. First your alarm goes off in the morning and you hit the snooze button. Then it goes off again, 15 minutes later, and you hit the snooze button once more. Then you finally get out of bed and get some coffee. Then the phone rings—well, you get the picture.

To help you overcome this roadblock to getting in the flow, try the 10-minute promise. Even if you do not feel like waking up early to trade, promise yourself that you will do it for just 10 minutes, and that if you still do not feel like it, then you can stop.

This strategy is a real winner. Most of the time you will not even notice that the 10 minutes are up because you will start to get caught up in the flow of what is going on.

FOCUS ON YOUR GOALS

Our final suggestion takes us full circle in this book and returns us to the topics we discussed in Chapters 1 and 2. In these chapters we encouraged you to write a mission statement and to set up some short-term and long-term trading goals. When we examine what it takes for us to be successful, happy, and in the flow, we find that focusing on goals and getting feedback are an essential part of the process.

Without a goal, it is very hard to concentrate on the task at hand, because we do not know what the task at hand is. What are we supposed to be doing with our time? A day with no goals is likely to be a day spent drifting aimlessly from one "urgent" phone call to the next "urgent" interruption. Setting goals and staying focused on them is the best method we know to get into the flow and to stay firmly focused on the here-and-now. Whatever you can do to stay focused on your goals is likely to help you achieve at a higher level than perhaps even you thought yourself capable of. Successful on-line trading athletes know to use such strategies as:

- Setting down their main objectives for the day first thing in the morning.
- Crossing off a goal as it is completed and moving on to the next one.
- Posting reminders of long-term goals in places they will be seen on a regular basis.
- Taking some time at the end of a day to write down some progress that has been made toward a long-term goal.
- Scheduling time to do some work without interruptions on important long-term goals.

- Setting deadlines for goals, and rewarding themselves when they meet the deadline.

As we end this chapter, it is important for you to understand that what it all comes down to is this: if you are in the batter's box or addressing the ball and thinking about what you could have done or what you already did you are missing out on what you can be doing. If you are going through the motions, fantasizing about what your batting average (profit and loss) is going to be if you go three for three (have three winning trades) then you are not going to be able to focus on the current situation.

By all means, if you are in a trade that is going your way, stay with it but avoid the temptation of pulling out your calculator and figuring out your profit and loss. Here is one last tip: keep everything in terms of "points" or "ticks." As soon as you start translating them into dollars, you distract yourself and leave the here-and-now of your game. We know it is tempting, especially if you are coming off a bad shot, but trust us, if you stray away from the here-and-now, winners can quickly become losers. The worst thing you can do as an online trading athlete is to turn a winner into a loser.

Focusing on the here-and-now requires a great deal of discipline. The thing to remember as an online trading athlete is that opportunities to make money will always be there. The trick is that when you decide to put your uniform on, you must focus on playing the game one trade at a time. If you find that you are looking ahead or stuck in the past, avoid getting discouraged. Remember, even all-stars like Tiger Woods, Mike Piazza, and Kobe Bryant make many, many errors in their game. So, learn from your mistakes and move on. Avoid the hope, wish, and pray technique. Focus on the can, do, and now.

ENJOYING THE MOMENT: PLAYING THE GAME ONE TRADE AT A TIME

- The basic principles of happiness

- Flow

    1. A challenging task we may succeed at
    2. The merging of action and awareness
    3. The task has clear goals
    4. The task provides immediate feedback
    5. Total concentration on the task at hand
    6. A feeling of control over your actions
    7. A loss of self-consciousness
    8. The transformation of time

- What happens when you enjoy the moment?

- Common ways out of flow

- Staying angry with yourself after a mistake

- Worrying about the future

- Unhappiness with the present

CHAPTER TEN

POSTGAME WRAP-UP

W e have both been around sports long enough to know that after the game, coaches like to pull their players into the dressing rooms for a final speech. But before we give you ours, we want to share with you John Wooden's "Pyramid of Success." As one of the all-time greatest coaches in sports history, he knew what it took to win.

A PYRAMID OF SUCCESS

Few teams in the history of sport can claim as much success as the UCLA men's basketball teams of the 1960s and 1970s. In the 12-year span between 1964 and 1975, the UCLA Bruins won 10 NCAA championships. That number is mind-boggling. Ten out of 12 national championships! The coach throughout that period was John Wooden.

Wooden is legendary as a coach, but what makes his legacy so interesting is that he always emphasized the

(continued)

mental, spiritual, and moral foundations of basketball success as much as the physical ones. You might say that he was an early sport psychologist. In his book, *They Call Me Coach*, Wooden says that:

> *[Y]ou cannot attain and maintain physical condition unless you are morally and mentally conditioned ... I tell my players that our team condition depends on two factors—how hard they work on the floor during practice and how well they behave between practices. You can neither attain nor maintain proper condition without working at both.*

A good coach can offer great insight into what it takes to attain success. A legendary coach such as Wooden deserves close study to see what he believed made the difference during his coaching career. Wooden's coaching philosophy is contained in his "Pyramid of Success," a model of the factors that lead to success that he developed while a teacher and coach at Central High School in South Bend, Indiana (see Figure F). He sometimes calls it "the only truly original thing I ever did." What we find remarkable about his model of success is that so much of it focuses on mental and social factors. Very little of it has to do with the actual skill level of the individual, although that component is a central factor in the pyramid.

Wooden emphasizes that success is a deeply personal matter, and can only ever really be measured by oneself. His definition of success, which is the pinnacle of his pyramid, reflects this thinking: "Success is the peace of mind that is a direct result of self-satisfaction in knowing you did your best to become the best you are capable of becoming." At the base of the pyramid

FIGURE **F**   **JOHN WOODEN'S "PYRAMID OF SUCCESS"**

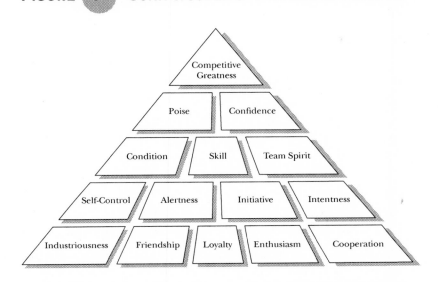

are the five building blocks on which everything else is based: (1) industriousness, (2) friendship, (3) loyalty, (4) enthusiasm, and (5) cooperation. Friendship and cooperation highlight the importance of getting along with others and helping others with sincerity and respect. Loyalty also includes loyalty to others, although Wooden also points out that it includes respect for oneself. Industriousness is the hard work that drives all successful people, and enthusiasm is the principle that you must have passion and love for what you do.

On the second of the pyramid's five rows are four more building blocks: (1) self-control, (2) alertness, (3) initiative, and (4) intentness. These are all mental factors that a sport psychologist would also call crucially important for success. The essence of self-control is balance: balance between mind and body and

(continued)

keeping one's emotions in balance. Alertness, which we have already discussed, is being able to spot weaknesses and do something to correct them. At the heart of what Wooden calls initiative, which is the drive to be good at what you do and the confidence to make a decision and act on it, is decision making. The fourth factor in this row is the interesting concept of intentness, which Wooden describes as the ability to resist temptation, and what we would call concentration.

On the third row of the pyramid are three more factors: (1) condition, (2) skill, and (3) team spirit. For Wooden, conditioning was not only physical but mental and spiritual as well. He spoke often of the importance of proper diet and proper rest. Skill includes all the technical mastery needed to excel in any given area, but it also incorporates the knowledge, or perhaps the instinct, to use the right skill at the right time. "Act quickly but don't hurry" was one of Wooden's favorite and paradoxical pieces of advice. Last, team spirit stands for the attitude of sacrificing personal glory for the good of the whole team. Wooden emphasized that not everyone on the team had to like each other, but that they should respect each other and be able to focus together on the basketball game.

On the pyramid's penultimate row are just two blocks—poise and confidence. Poise is defined as just being yourself. It is something we always recognize in those who are truly happy—they are comfortable with who they are. For Wooden, confidence stemmed from preparation. He wanted his players to respect their opponents but not fear them, and to be confident but not cocky. "Failure to prepare is preparing to fail" is another of his pithy summaries of this building block.

Finally, on the top of the pyramid is competitive greatness, defined as the love of battle. For Wooden, competition was the ultimate test of everything he taught, and he looked forward to it and looked for players who enjoyed it. He recognized the possibility of failure, but he did not dwell on it because he believed that by following his game plan, success was the likely outcome.

Certainly the results he achieved support his faith. By the time he quit coaching in 1975, Wooden had been named "Coach of the Year" six times, and was known everywhere as "The Wizard of Westwood." As of today, he is the only person to be inducted into the Basketball Hall of Fame as both a player and a coach.

As you can see, Wooden's "Pyramid of Success" is a model for achieving performance excellence. His coaching philosophy parallels some of the winning concepts that we have presented throughout this book. To achieve greatness, one must learn from the "greats."

Now it is time to wind things down but before you head to the showers, let us do a brief wrap-up of what we have covered in this book. We have been privileged to act as your coaches on the mental aspects of trading, and we hope we have convinced you that you should approach the game as an online trading athlete.

Although each chapter covered a lot of material, it might be helpful first to go back over each chapter and emphasize one key point as a reminder of what you have learned. If you only apply the following key point for each chapter, you will still be far ahead of the game compared to most traders who do not know about sport psychology and how to achieve performance excellence.

CHAPTER 1. THE PERSONAL TRADING MISSION STATEMENT

If the market has been running against you, if you feel tired and depressed, if things are not going too well in your personal life, what keeps you going? What is to prevent you from just giving up and getting a nice safe job flipping burgers at McDonalds? The answer is—your personal trading mission statement. It is a summary of who you are, what you want from your trading experience, and what you are committed to.

CHAPTER 2. EFFECTIVE GOAL-SETTING

There are few occupations that have as many options as that of the online trading athlete. Your areas of expertise and specialization are limited only by your imagination and courage. In order to stay focused and productive in such an environment, you must become truly excellent at the art of setting goals. You must know why goals work, what makes a good goal, and how to break your long-term dreams down into short-term reality.

CHAPTER 3. CONFIDENCE AND BODY LANGUAGE

We hope we surprised you into thinking seriously about the effect that your posture, your gestures, and your overall tone

have on your general level of confidence as a trader. It is not
a matter of fooling yourself into being confident, it is a matter of starting out with a bold, confident approach of looking and acting assertive, and then allowing your feelings to
catch up to and get in line with your actions.

CHAPTER 4. A POSITIVE TRADING ATTITUDE

Can you look at your work as an online trading athlete and
be critical but not negative? That is the key to developing a
long-term positive trading attitude (PTA). Being critical
means looking at yourself in the mirror and honestly identifying those areas that need improvement. The tendency is
to be negative about the fact that you have some weaknesses,
but if you adopt a PTA instead, you will look at those weaknesses as an opportunity to get better. In the long run, you
want to be the best online trading athlete you can be.

CHAPTER 5. USING ENERGIZING SELF-TALK TO REDUCE THE PRESSURES OF TRADING

We introduced the concept of self-talk in Chapter 4 when
we explained the PTA. Self-talk is that internal dialogue we
have with ourselves, especially when our performance is being evaluated. We demonstrated that the source of all the
pressure we feel as online trading athletes comes from our

self-talk. It is completely our choice as to how much pressure we feel every day. By learning to use energizing self-talk regularly, we can overcome our tendency to feel stressed out and instead learn to stay motivated and energized.

CHAPTER 6. HOW TO AVOID TRADING FOR REVENGE

There are two principal emotional reactions to trading failures. We can become anxious and fearful, or we can become frustrated and angry. In this chapter we examined what happens to traders who get angry at the market. Very often, traders try to get rid of their anger by seeking revenge. There is a strong tendency to want to "settle the score" and "get even." Trading for revenge against an impervious force like the market usually ends in disaster and heartbreak, and is the quickest way we know of entering into early retirement from being an online trading athlete.

CHAPTER 7. LEARNING TO RELAX AND CALM DOWN WHEN ANXIOUS

In this chapter we examine anxiety, the second most common reaction to trading failures. It is normal to get nervous when trading a great deal of money, but too much anxiety can lead to panic and a total meltdown for the online trading athlete. To prevent anxiety from becoming excessive, we showed you how to relax properly and deeply, and how to use effective relaxation strategies when you really need them—in the heat of battle.

CHAPTER 8. TUNING IN TO YOUR EFFECTIVE PERFORMANCE CUES

There are always many distractions for the serious online trading athlete. Trying to block these distractions out can be a time-consuming waste of energy. Instead, we showed you how to identify and tune in to the few critical factors that ultimately determine your success. By learning to focus your attention on what is important you free up your energies in order to perform to your fullest potential.

CHAPTER 9. STAYING FOCUSED ON THE HERE-AND-NOW

Past mistakes make you angry, and worries about what will happen to the market make you anxious, so it is only by learning to focus on the here-and-now that you can become a successful online trading athlete. When you are fully focused on doing what you enjoy, you are in the flow, and it is then that you are most likely to make successful decisions, free from doubts and insecurities. We tend to perform our best when we are truly happy, but you do not wait around hoping to feel good before you jump into the trading day. In this chapter we showed you that making a commitment to action, to taking the first step, no matter how small, and playing the game one trade at a time is what leads to long-term success.

Now that we have had a chance to review the game, let us look ahead to the remaining schedule. What do you need to work on as a player to keep improving? To help you focus in on your strengths and weaknesses, we have put together the following self-evaluation. Answer the questions, add up your scores, and we will identify skills you excel at and which you need to keep working on to be an exceptional online trading athlete. Ready? Here we go.

ONLINE TRADING ATHLETE SELF-EVALUATION

Answer all of the following questions by circling either "Yes" or "No."

GOAL SETTING

This first set of 10 questions is on *goal setting*. Answer them about how you are generally.

1. I have specific goals for every trading day.
    YES   NO
2. When I set a goal for myself, I make a plan for reaching it.
    YES   NO
3. I set trading goals that have nothing to do with how much I will make.
    YES   NO
4. When I set a goal, I evaluate how well I do in reaching it.
    YES   NO
5. I ask for feedback from others to see how much progress I am making.
    YES   NO
6. When facing a difficult project, I set realistic but challenging goals.
    YES   NO
7. I set very clear, specific, and measurable goals for myself.
    YES   NO

8. I spend time planning how I will reach my trading goals.

    YES   NO

9. I regularly evaluate and document whether I have made progress in reaching my trading goals.

    YES   NO

10. I set short-term goals to help me reach my long-term goals.

    YES   NO

SCORING

Give yourself 1 point for every question you answered YES. This will give you a total score between 0 and 10.

10 points	Congratulations! You are an ace at goal setting. Chapter 2 should be a reinforcement of your good habits.
7–9 points	You are usually an effective goal-setter, but at times you know you can do better. Chapter 2 has some useful suggestions for you.
3–6 points	You are an average goal-setter. Chapter 2 will be an important resource for you as you strive to become a better online trading athlete.
0–2 points	Being able to set effective goals is a real weakness for you. You should start reading Chapter 2 immediately, and make it a priority to improve your goal-setting skills.

CONFIDENCE

Now answer the following 10 questions on *confidence.*

11. When faced with a problem, I imagine successful solutions.

    YES   NO

12. I know how to stay calm and look confident when trading.
    YES   NO
13. I visualize successfully when dealing with unexpected market conditions.
    YES   NO
14. Before I sit down in my trading stadium, I imagine being successful.
    YES   NO
15. When things are not going well at work, I take a time out to regroup.
    YES   NO
16. Before trading, I imagine successful past performances.
    YES   NO
17. When things get difficult throughout the day, I know how to stay upbeat.
    YES   NO
18. I know how to get myself out of a slump.
    YES   NO
19. I have a routine I try to stick to during a trading day.
    YES   NO
20. I imagine myself screwing up in pressure situations.
    YES   NO

SCORING

Give yourself 1 point for every question you answered YES and 1 point if you answered NO to question 20. This will give you a total score between 0 and 10.

10 points   Congratulations! You know how to be and stay confident. Chapter 3 should be a reinforcement of your good habits.

7–9 points   You are usually confident, but at times your self-doubts hamper your effectiveness. Chapter 3 has some useful suggestions for you.

3–6 points   You have average confidence. Chapter 3 will be an important resource for you as you strive to become a better online trading athlete.

0–2 points   Staying confident is a real weakness for you. You should start reading Chapter 3 immediately, and make it a priority to improve your trading confidence.

POSITIVE TRADING ATTITUDE

Now answer the following 10 questions about your *positive trading attitude* (PTA).

21. I keep my thoughts positive in difficult trading situations.

     YES   NO

22. I know what to say to myself in tough trading situations to help me do my best.

     YES   NO

23. I know how to handle it if I start to have thoughts of failure.

     YES   NO

24. When I start to be too critical of myself, I know how to stop and think productively instead.

     YES   NO

25. I regularly practice ways to keep my thoughts positive in challenging situations.

     YES   NO

26. I do not let negative thoughts stop me from doing my best.

     YES   NO

27. I think positively even when problems arise.

     YES   NO

28. If I do not feel like doing something, I know how to talk myself into getting started.

     YES   NO

29. I am honest with myself in identifying my strengths.
    YES   NO
30. I am honest with myself in identifying my weak-
    nesses.
    YES   NO

SCORING

Give yourself 1 point for every question you answered YES.
This will give you a total score between 0 and 10.

10 points	Congratulations! You have an excellent PTA. Chapter 4 should be a reinforcement of your good habits.
7–9 points	You usually have a PTA, but at times you allow negative thoughts to creep in. Chapter 4 has some useful suggestions for you.
3–6 points	Your trading attitude is inconsistent. Chapter 4 will be an important resource for you as you strive to become a better online trading athlete.
0–2 points	Having a PTA is a real weakness for you. You should start reading Chapter 4 immediately, and make it a priority to improve your trading attitude.

ENERGIZING

Now answer the following 10 questions on *energizing*.

31. I know good ways to keep my energy level high.
    YES   NO
32. I can get myself psyched up for important situations
    when I need to appear at my best.
    YES   NO

33. I can increase my energy level immediately if I am tired or fatigued.
    YES   NO
34. I can psych myself up for the trading day if I need to.
    YES   NO
35. I take regular breaks to reenergize during the trading day.
    YES   NO
36. I keep my thoughts positive when I am having an "off-day."
    YES   NO
37. I exercise regularly.
    YES   NO
38. I know just how much energy I need to perform at my best.
    YES   NO
39. I maintain consistent eating and sleeping habits during the week.
    YES   NO
40. I can raise my energy level when I am feeling worn out during the week.
    YES   NO

SCORING

Give yourself 1 point for every question you answered YES. This will give you a total score between 0 and 10.

10 points	Congratulations! You are very good at energizing when the pressure is on. Chapter 5 should be a reinforcement of your good habits.
7–9 points	You usually stay energized in pressure situations, but at times you get overwhelmed. Chapter 5 has some useful suggestions for you.

3–6 points   Your ability to stay energized and positive is in-
               consistent. Chapter 5 will be an important re-
               source for you as you strive to become a better
               online trading athlete.

0–2 points   Staying energized in the face of adversity is a real
               weakness for you. You should start reading
               Chapter 5 immediately, and make it a priority to
               improve your ability to energize.

ANGER MANAGEMENT

Now answer the following 10 questions dealing with *anger management*.

41. When someone criticizes my trading, I feel miserable, often for days.
    YES   NO

42. When I am angry, I feel better if I try to make back my losses quickly.
    YES   NO

43. When things are going badly, my emotions get out of control.
    YES   NO

44. It takes a lot of effort for me to keep my emotions in check.
    YES   NO

45. I need to develop an effective way to deal with my frustration.
    YES   NO

46. My emotions stop me from doing my best in high-pressure situations.
    YES   NO

47. If I encounter a setback, I can rebound and still perform effectively.
    YES   NO

48. I do not get flustered or freeze up when I am caught in
    a fast market and it is going against me.
    YES   NO
49. I am flexible enough to alter my trading strategy when
    I have to.
    YES   NO
50. I am able to make quick decisions and not second-guess
    myself.
    YES   NO

Scoring

Give yourself 1 point for every question you answered NO
from 41 to 46, and 1 point for every YES from 47 to 50. This
will give you a total score between 0 and 10.

10 points	Congratulations! You never trade for revenge. Chapter 6 should be a reinforcement of your good habits.
7–9 points	It is not often that you allow yourself to get upset at the market, but at times you do get frustrated or angry. Chapter 6 has some useful suggestions for you.
3–6 points	You are sometimes guilty of trading for revenge. Chapter 6 will be an important resource for you as you strive to become a better online trading athlete.
0–2 points	Your habit of trading for revenge is a real weakness for you. You should start reading Chapter 6 immediately, and make it a priority to stay under control when the market goes against you.

Pressure

Now answer the following 10 questions dealing with *pressure*.

51. I know how to deal with the butterflies in my stomach if I am making an important trade.

    YES   NO

52. If I am too nervous or uptight, I know how to relax and calm down.

    YES   NO

53. I regularly practice a way to relax and stay calm in pressure situations.

    YES   NO

54. I handle stressful situations in a productive and professional way.

    YES   NO

55. I perform at my best even when the pressure is greatest and others are evaluating my performance.

    YES   NO

56. When trading, I sometimes freeze and forget what I am supposed to do or how to do it.

    YES   NO

57. While trading my mind sometimes races, with too many thoughts competing for attention.

    YES   NO

58. I sometimes figure out my profit and loss while I am in the middle of a trade.

    YES   NO

59. Sometimes I panic and make bad decisions under pressure.

    YES   NO

60. If I get too tense and uptight during the trading day, I can unwind and loosen up.

    YES   NO

SCORING

Give yourself 1 point for every question you answered YES from 51 to 55, and 1 point for every NO from 56 to 60. This will give you a total score between 0 and 10.

10 points	Congratulations! You know how to stay calm under pressure. Chapter 7 should be a reinforcement of your good habits.
7–9 points	You usually stay relaxed while trading, but at times you feel anxious. Chapter 7 has some useful suggestions for you.
3–6 points	You experience too much anxiety at times while trading. Chapter 7 will be an important resource for you as you strive to become a better online trading athlete.
0–2 points	Getting overanxious and panicking is a real weakness for you. You should start reading Chapter 7 immediately, and make it a priority to improve your ability to relax in stressful situations.

CONCENTRATION

Now answer the following 10 questions dealing with *concentration.*

61. I am good at maintaining my concentration during a long trading day.
    YES   NO
62. When I make a mistake in an important trading situation, I can quickly get my concentration back on track.
    YES   NO
63. When I am distracted while trading, I quickly forget about it and get back to work.
    YES   NO
64. I am able to stay focused on a task for as long as necessary.
    YES   NO
65. I regularly practice ways to increase my concentration.
    YES   NO

66. When things get hectic while trading, I know how to keep it simple.
    YES   NO
67. I can stay calm if I make a mistake.
    YES   NO
68. I know how to pay attention to the important aspects of my trading.
    YES   NO
69. When I am "in the market," I use performance cues to get my head in the game.
    YES   NO
70. I sometimes get so distracted and confused when I am trading that I forget to pay attention to important details.
    YES   NO

SCORING

Give yourself 1 point for every question you answered YES from 61 to 69, and 1 point if you answered NO to question 70. This will give you a total score between 0 and 10.

10 points	Congratulations! You are a master of concentration. Chapter 8 should be a reinforcement of your good habits.
7–9 points	You usually stay focused while trading, but at times you get distracted. Chapter 8 has some useful suggestions for you.
3–6 points	Your concentration while trading is inconsistent. Chapter 8 will be an important resource for you as you strive to become a better online trading athlete.
0–2 points	One of your major weaknesses is your lack of ability to focus and concentrate. You should start reading Chapter 8 immediately, and make it a priority to improve your concentration.

FLOW

Now answer the following 10 questions dealing with *flow*.

71. I really enjoy trading.

    YES   NO

72. I prepare carefully for important challenges in my trading life.

    YES   NO

73. I document the situation (market condition/stock sector/long-short/size of trade) when I am not trading at the top of my game.

    YES   NO

74. I seem to be able to get into a smooth flow when I am trading.

    YES   NO

75. I have a regular way I warm up or prepare for trading.

    YES   NO

76. In pressure situations, I often react well and instinctively.

    YES   NO

77. I coordinate my trading style/theory to capitalize on my strengths and limit my weaknesses.

    YES   NO

78. I am always willing to try a new approach if my current game plan is consistently not working.

    YES   NO

79. I have to think a long time about all my trades—I cannot get in a rhythm where it just happens.

    YES   NO

80. I often overanalyze my work instead of trusting myself to do well.

    YES   NO

Scoring

Give yourself 1 point for every question you answered YES
from 71 to 78, and 1 point for every NO from 79 to 80. This
will give you a total score between 0 and 10.

10 points	Congratulations! You are always well prepared to stay in the flow. Chapter 9 should be a reinforcement of your good habits.
7–9 points	You are usually in the flow while trading, but at times you lack preparation. Chapter 9 has some useful suggestions for you.
3–6 points	You do not feel in the flow often enough during the trading day. Chapter 9 will be an important resource for you as you strive to become a better online trading athlete.
0–2 points	You rarely experience the flow as a trader. You should start reading Chapter 9 immediately, and make it a priority to improve your ability to stay in the flow and the here-and-now.

That just about does it for the locker-room speech. Now it
is time for the final pep talk. After this you will be equipped
to get yourself back in the game.

First of all, remember your mission. If you went through
the whole game without taking the time to write it down and
you were consistently making great contact off the pitcher
(the market) then we tip our cap to you and wish you the best.

However, if you found that your timing was off, your
pitch selection was horrible, and that you were on a roller
coaster ride, well, then maybe you ought to call a time out,
make a commitment, identify why you are trading and put
it on paper.

Next, discipline. We have said it once and we will say it
again, if you do not have discipline, then do not even bother

picking up your bat and stepping up to the plate. Home runs are nice but if you are hitting .108 with 15 homeruns, we do not think you are going to be in the lineup for very long. Think batting titles rather than solo 500-foot shots.

Maintain your confidence. Keep that positive trading attitude. Mistakes are part of the game. Going 0 for 5 is part of the game. Instead of counting how many hits you have, count your quality at bats (trades). Remember, it is possible to lose money on a good trade. The real all-stars in this game are confident and consistent.

Follow the six steps to goal setting: (1) achievable, (2) measurable, (3) controllable, (4) positive, (5) strategic, and (6) flexible. If your current goal is missing one of these six things, then call a time-out, and reevaluate your goals. Focus on the process of reaching your goals rather than the outcome.

If there is anything that we have learned in our years of working with traders and athletes, it is that the market (the game) is bigger and badder than all of us. It has been around a lot longer than we have and it will still be here long after we are gone. When your ego is bruised because of that trade that went against you for no apparent reason, just remember that if you fall prey to trading for revenge, the only thing that you are going to end up doing is giving back your hard-earned month.

Avoid falling into the trap. Be smart. Take a time-out. Recover. Refocus. Use your self-talk and smile. Shake it off. Play this game on your terms. Stay in control, follow your game plan, and swing at quality pitches. Instead of fighting the market, read it, follow it, and ride it like a wave. Rather than trying to figure it out, respect it, give it some space, let it breath. Do not worry—it is not going anywhere. It will still be there tomorrow.

Stay balanced. When a hitter steps to the plate, the two most important things that he has with him are his body and his mind. For the hitter, as well as the online trading athlete, both of these things need to be at peak performance in order to achieve success. The keys to staying balanced and at the top of your game are proper nutrition, which keeps you physically ready, and adequate rest, which recharges your mental batteries.

Play the game one trade at a time. Continually remind yourself to stay in the here-and-now. When the market opens and the umpire yells "play ball," focus on this moment, this trade. Avoid reliving the past or dreaming of the future. The past is over and the future will be here soon enough. Stay disciplined. Make this moment the quality at-bat (trade) that you have practiced for and remember to always keep your eye on the ball and your head in the game!

We enjoyed sharing our knowledge of sport psychology and trading with you in *The Trading Athlete: Winning the Mental Game of Online Trading*.

By the way, anyone know what the final score was?

————— ◆ —————

EXTRA INNINGS

This section is filled with pointers, strategies, tips, and worksheets to help the online trading athlete win the mental game of trading. It is arranged in five parts.

Part I.   Learning Relaxation Strategies
Part II.   Pregame Motivational Statements
Part III. The Focused Trader's Rules to Trade By
Part IV.   Designing Your Winning Trading Stadium
Part V.   Worksheets

All of these concepts are designed to supplement the main part of this book while giving you a little something extra that you can put immediately into your game plan. Have fun with it and remember: stay focused!

PART I. LEARNING RELAXATION STRATEGIES

The following section shows you some simple skills that you can put into your game plan that will help you reduce nervousness and prevent panic from affecting your performance. We have found that traders like to keep a journal as they work their way through this part of the book. By writing down any ideas that come to mind they can customize these skills for future use.

WHEN AM I ANXIOUS?

Take a moment or two to identify which events cause you the most problems and rate the level of anxiety from 1 (completely calm) to 5 (panic).

Situation	Calm		Anxious		Panic
1. Making a big trade	1	2	3	4	5
2. Taking a short position	1	2	3	4	5
3. Placing a market order	1	2	3	4	5
4. Waiting for earnings reports	1	2	3	4	5
5. Anticipating economic releases	1	2	3	4	5
6. Trading next to someone else	1	2	3	4	5
7. Waiting for the market to open	1	2	3	4	5
8. Trading on my own	1	2	3	4	5
9. _____	1	2	3	4	5
10. _____	1	2	3	4	5

Note: If we missed anything, feel free to add your own in the spaces above.

Now, select one or two of the above situations that you scored a 4 or above, and circle the feelings you have during those anxious times.

- Difficulty breathing
- Nausea
- Sweaty hands or face

- Dizziness
- A numb feeling in certain body parts
- Extreme anger
- Sleeping difficulties
- Overwhelming fatigue when it is not time to sleep
- Difficulty concentrating
- Irritability or excessive anger
- Rapid or irregular heartbeat
- _____
- _____

Note: If there are other feelings you experience, make sure to add them in the blank spaces above.

The purpose of this exercise is to help you identify what makes you become anxious and to understand how it impacts you as an online trading athlete. Once you are able to clearly identify these two things, then you will be in a position to deal with them by using some of the proactive strategies we show you throughout this Appendix. It may be worthwhile to write down what you discovered about yourself from the above exercise so that you can revisit it in a couple of weeks and see how much progress you have made. Now that you have identified what causes you stress and anxiety as an online trading athlete, let us begin to do something about it.

RELAXATION STRATEGIES

Creating the Right Environment

For each relaxation method that will be described (circular breathing, muscle relaxation, visualization) utilize the following hints while you are practicing each method.

- *Quiet time and place*: Choose a time and place you will not be disturbed for at least 15 minutes.
- *Loose clothing*: Choose clothing that helps you relax (sweatpants, boxers, and so on) and do not forget to take off eyeglasses, shoes, belts, and watches.
- *Comfortable position*: Pick a comfortable position. It might be lying on your back on a firm, supportive surface or sitting in a chair with your knees comfortably apart, palms resting on thighs—whatever works for you.

Now that you understand what kind of environment you should be in when you practice relaxation, take 10 to 15 minutes in the next week to try each of the following relaxation methods out. Later, as you become more skilled in using these relaxation strategies, you will be able to use them quickly, in a pressure situation, anytime you need it. But remember, in order to become skilled at using them, you need to put some quality time into practicing them.

If you have never used relaxation techniques before then it will seem awkward the first few times, but what new skill is not awkward when you first try it out? Think about the first time you were taught how to grip a golf club properly or tried dribbling a basketball with your other hand. How did that feel? Uncomfortable, right? Of course it it did, but once you spent some quality time on the driving range or on the court, it became second nature and you saw improvement in your game. The same is true for relaxation strategies. If you stick with them, we are confident that you will see a difference in your performance as an online trading athlete.

One last pointer before we begin is that sometimes a skill that does not appeal to you initially may turn out to be the most valuable weapon in your arsenal. Besides, what do you have to lose? After all, you picked up this book because